THE BOOK O BALTIMORE ORIOLES LISTS

by DAVID PUGH

Illustrations by
MIKE RICIGLIANO

Foreword by
DAN RODRICKS

AMERICAN LITERARY PRESS
Baltimore, Maryland

The Book of Baltimore Orioles Lists

Library of Congress
Cataloging in Publication Data
ISBN 1-56167-523-7

Published by

American Literary Press, Inc.
8019 Belair Road, Suite 10
Baltimore, Maryland 21236

Manufactured in the United States of America

TABLE OF CONTENTS

Foreword *by Dan Rodricks* ....*xiii*

A Fan's History of the Baltimore Orioles *by Linda Geeson* ....*xv*

Chapter 1 • Names *1*

The Six Most Common Oriole First Names 2
The Seven Most Common Oriole Last Names 2
The Seven Most Common Oriole Middle Names 3
The Seven Most Common Names That Orioles Go By..3
The Eight Players Whose Name They Go By And Last Name Are On The
    Lists Of Most Common Names...3
Two Players Whose First, Middle And Last Names, As Well As The Names
    They Go By, Are On The Lists Of Most Common Names 4
The All-Bob Team 4
The All-David-Dave-Davey Team...4
Three Orioles With The Same First And Last Names 5
Six Orioles With Kooky Middle Names 5
13 Orioles Better Known By Their Middle Names...6
Six Oriole "Berts" 6
Five Orioles Who Shortened Their Names 6
Seven First, Middle And Last Names...7
Six Oriole Catchers Whose Last Names Begin And End With The Same Letter 7
Groups Of Players With The Same Last Name Who Played On The Same Team 8
The Orioles-With-Girlie-Names Team 8
Sounds The Same, Spelled Differently 9
The All-Alliterative Team 9
Five Orioles With Fishy Names..9
Three Birds With Birdie Names...9
Eleven Orioles With Job Names 10
Three Orioles With Car Names 10
Ten Orioles With Colorful Names 11
Three Orioles With Christmas Names..11
Four Orioles With "Spirited" Names..11
Too Bad Bob Watson Never Was An Oriole 11
Five Orioles With Team Names 12
15 Orioles Better Known By Their Nicknames 12
Four Pairs Of Orioles With The Same Nicknames 12
Three Orioles Nicknamed "Moose" 13
Seven Orioles With Nicknames Based On Their Physical Attributes....................13
Ten Orioles With Animal Nicknames...14
Three Orioles With Nicknames Based On Their Personalities 14
Nine Before And After Names..14
With Apologies To ESPN's Chris Berman...15
Two Right-Handed Orioles Submariners Whose First Names Are Dick
    And Last Names Start With "H" 15
Three Orioles Who Should Have Been Marx Brothers 16

The First-Name-Ends-In-"O" Team *16*
Top Ten Oriole Fab Four Hits Plus One *17*
Seven From Mick And Keith (Not Tettleton And Moreland)......................................*18*
Four Beach Boys Of Summer *18*
Ten Rock And Roll Orioles *18*
Ten All-Stars Of The Silver Screen *19*
A Bobby Bo Nanza *19*
Birdland Or TV Land *19*
Eight, Eight, Eight Names In One..*19*
Seven Cereal Killers..*20*
My Fair (Or Foul) Lady *20*
20 Fun Name Combinations *21*
Answer To Eight, Eight, Eight Names In One...*21*
The Nine Shortest Last Names *22*
The Seven Longest Last Names *22*
The Only Three Players Named John To Ever Play Second Base For The Orioles...........*22*
The Only Three Players Named Jeff To Ever Play Second Base For The Orioles
    Who Also Happen To Be The Only Three Players Named Jeff To Ever Play
    Shortstop For The Orioles *23*
The Most-Popular-Name-For-Each-Position Team...*23*
Billy's Who Played Second Base, Shortstop And Third Base For The Orioles...................*23*
The All-Presidents Team...*24*
Ricig's Ten Favorite Orioles To Draw..*25*

Chapter 2 • Numbers **26**
The Twelve Most Used Numbers..*27*
Five *Other* Orioles Who Wore Number 5 ....*27*
Six Numbers Worn By Only One Oriole *27*
The All Number-17 Team *28*
Two Orioles Who Wore Three Different Numbers During One Season *28*
17 Players Who Wore The Same Number For Ten Seasons Or More *29*
Seven Non-Players Who Wore The Same Number For Ten Seasons Or More *29*
The Seven Orioles Who Wore The Most Different Numbers.......................................*30*
13 Orioles Who Wore Lucky Number 13 ....*31*
The Only Five Numbers Worn By Orioles Pitching Coaches *32*
Two Orioles Who Wore Two Different Numbers While With The Orioles,
    Yet Appeared in Just One Game *32*
The Five Uniform Numbers Retired By The Orioles *32*
The Last Five Players To Wear The Retired Numbers Before The Retirees Did *33*
Two Orioles Who Wore *Two* Numbers That Were Eventually Retired *33*
Seven Oriole Catchers Who Wore Number 10 ....*33*
Three Orioles Who Wore Number 15 And Later Managed In The Bigs *33*
Three Orioles Who Wore Number 25 And Later Managed In The Bigs *34*
Same Last Name, Same Number *34*
The All Prime Number Team..*34*
Two Maryland-Born Oriole Shortstops Who Wore Number 8 ....*35*
Ten Oriole-Magic Things About The Number 268 ....*35*
Ten Numbers Worn By Three Orioles In The Same Season In The 1950s...................*36*
Four Orioles Who Wore Number 34 During The 1955 Season.....................................*36*

Five Numbers Worn By Three Orioles In The Same Season Since The 1950s......................37
The Identical-Double-Digit Team..37

Chapter 3 • Home Runs **38**

Six Orioles Who Hit Three Consecutive Home Runs In A Game..39
Seven Orioles Who Hit Three Non-Consecutive Home Runs In A Game...........................39
Two Games In Which The Orioles Hit Four Home Runs In One Inning 39
Six Games In Which The Orioles Hit Three Consecutive Home Runs In One Inning......40
Three Former Oriole Pitchers Who Gave Up Eddie Murray's First Three
    Career Home Runs..40
Two Oriole Pitchers Who Gave Up Three Home Runs To Eddie Murray 40
Three Oriole Pitchers Who Gave Up Home Runs To Roger Maris In 1961 41
Six Orioles Who Hit A Home Run In Their First Major League At Bat
    (Though Not Necessarily With The Orioles) 41
Four Orioles Who Hit Home Runs From Both Sides Of The Plate In The Same Game....41
Two Games In Which The Orioles Hit Back-To-Back Pinch-Hit Home Runs....................42
Two Games In Which The Orioles' First Two Batters Hit Home Runs 42
Two Innings In Which Both Cal And Bill Ripken Homered..42
Four Orioles To Hit 20 Home Runs And Steal 20 Bases In A Season 42
Two Famous Home Runs Given Up By Oriole Pitchers 43
Four Orioles Who Hit Home Runs In The Seventh Inning On May 17, 1967.....................43
Eight Oriole Home Run Events That Happened On August 26th..43
Six Orioles Who Hit Grand Slams On August 26th...44
Most Popular Days Of The Month For Orioles Grand Slams...44
Least Popular Day Of The Month For Orioles Grand Slams...45
Six Days When Two Oriole Grand Slams Were Hit 45
Three Times Oriole Grand Slams Were Hit On Consecutive Days 45
Eleven Orioles Who Hit Pinch-Hit Grand Slams..46
Seven Orioles Who Are All-Time Home Run Leaders For Their Home State 46
Six Orioles Who Are Second On The All-Time Home Run List For Their Home State 47
Three Orioles In The Top Five All-Time Home Run Leaders Whose Last Name
    Begins With The Letter "R" 47
24 Orioles Pitchers Who Hit Regular Season Home Runs...47
Four Oriole Pitchers Who Hit Two Home Runs In One Game With Either
    The Tigers Or The Orioles..48
Two Oriole Pitchers Who Hit Post-Season Home Runs 48

Chapter 4 • Pitchers & Pitching **49**

Twelve Orioles Team Pitching Triple Crown Winners 50
Five Oriole No-Hitters 50
Two Orioles No-Hitters Spoiled In The Ninth Inning By The Twins Cesar Tovar
    In 1969..51
Eleven Oriole 20-Game Winners 51
Five Great Pitchers Who Lost At Least 20 Games To The Orioles 52
Six Oriole Pitchers With Impressive Single-Season Winning Streaks 52
Four Orioles Pitchers To Go Undefeated In A Season (With At Least Five Wins).............52
Four Orioles Who Pitched A Shutout In Their First Major League Start............................53
Four California Angels Struck Out By Mike Cuellar In The Fourth Inning
    On May 29, 1970 53

Five Non-Pitchers Who Pitched For The Orioles 54
Three Major League Pitching Records Shared By An Oriole 54
Five Oriole Pitchers Who Led The League In Shutouts 54
Five Oriole Pitchers Who Led The League With The Fewest Hits Plus Walks
     Per Nine-Inning Game 55
Seven Oriole Pitchers Who Led The League In Won-Lost Percentage 55
Four Oriole Pitchers Who Led The League In Complete Games..55
Four Oriole Pitchers Who Led The League In Games Pitched 56
Three Oriole Pitchers Who Led The League In Saves...56
Three Oriole Pitchers Who Led The League In Opponents Batting Average.....................56
Six Oriole Pitchers Who Led The League In Opponents On Base Percentage....................56
Nine Oriole Pitchers Who Led The League (Or Tied For The League Lead) In Wins.......57
Three Oriole Pitchers Who Led The League In Earned Run Average 57
Five Pitching Categories Led By Oriole Pitchers In 1970 57
Six Pitching Categories Led By Oriole Pitchers In 1979 58
Four A.L. or Major League Pitching Categories Led By Scott Erickson In 1998................58
Eight Oriole Pitchers Who Hit Triples 58
18 Switch-Hitting Pitchers...59
Twelve Oriole Starting Pitchers Named Mike..59

Chapter 5 • All-Stars 60
19 Oriole All-Star Starters..61
Five Oriole All-Star Game MVPs 61
26 Oriole All-Star Non-Starters...62
21 Oriole All-Stars Who Didn't Get A Chance To Play 63
Five Oriole All-Stars Who Didn't Attend Due To Injury..63
Four Orioles Who Homered In An All-Star Game..64
Five Orioles Who Were All-Stars Before, During And After Their Stint
     With The Orioles 64
Eleven Former, Current And Future Orioles Who Were 1961 All-Stars 65
13 1998 Orioles Who Were Ever All-Stars (Big Deal!)..65
Eleven Former, Current And Future Orioles Who Were 1983 All-Stars 66
14 Former, Current And Future Orioles Who Were 1991 All-Stars......................................66
Four Orioles Who Have Appeared In Movies 67

Chapter 6 • Awards & Halls of Fame 68
Four Oriole A.L. MVP's...69
Four Oriole A.L. Cy Young Award Winners (Baseball Writers Association
     Of America)..69
Seven Oriole A.L. Rookies Of The Year 69
Two Players Who Won Rookie Of The Year And Later Won Two MVP Awards 69
Eight Cy Young Award Also-Rans 70
Eleven MVP Award Also-Rans 71
Nine BBWAA Rookie Of The Year Also-Rans 71
Three Oriole A.L. Rookie Pitchers Of The Year (The Sporting News)...............................72
Three Oriole A.L. Players Of The Year (TSN) 72
Two Oriole Major League Players Of The Year (TSN) 72
Four Oriole A.L. Pitchers Of The Year (TSN) 72
Four Oriole Roberto Clemente Award Winners...72

Three Oriole World Series MVPs 73
Two Years In Which Orioles Have Finished 1-2-3 In Major Award Balloting.....................73
Four Orioles Who Won Comeback Player Of The Year 73
Two Orioles Who Were Puerto Rican League MVPs 73
27 Most Valuable Orioles..74
Twelve Oriole Gold Glove Winners (57 Gold Gloves) 75
Eight Oriole Team Triple Crown Winners 75
The Orioles All Award-Winners Team..76
Nine Orioles In The Baseball Hall Of Fame..77
Twelve Orioles Who Received Hall Of Fame Votes But Didn't Quite
    Make Cooperstown 77
36 Oriole Hall Of Fame Members...78
Ten Orioles In Latin American Halls Of Fame...79

Chapter 7 • League Leaders *80*

Four Orioles Who Led The League In Runs Batted In 81
Three Orioles Who Led The League In Runs Scored 81
Three Orioles Who Led The League In Slugging Percentage...................................81
Four Oriole Catchers Who Led The League In Fielding Percentage 81
Two Oriole First Basemen Who Led The League In Fielding Percentage 81
Six Oriole Second Basemen Who Led The League In Fielding Percentage.............82
Three Oriole Shortstops Who Led The League In Fielding Percentage...................82
13 Years In Which An Oriole Third Baseman Led The League In Fielding Percentage 82
The All-Led-The-League-In-Fielding-Percentage-In-1963 Infield 83
Three Oriole Outfielders Who Led The League In Fielding Percentage...................83
Six League Batting Categories Led By Frank Robinson In 1966...............................84
Three Orioles Who Lead The Majors In Games Played At Their Positions 84
Two Dubious Categories With Orioles At Number One And Number Two In 1998.........84

Chapter 8 • Achievements *85*

Nine All-Time Third Base Records Held By Brooks Robinson 86
Two All-Time Orioles Batting Totals With Brooks In First Place And Cal
    In Second Place...86
Five All-Time Orioles Batting Totals With Cal In First Place And Brooks
    In Second Place...86
Seven All-Time Orioles Batting Records With Eddie Murray In Third Place
    (Behind Brooks And Cal) 87
Four Orioles Who Hit Four Extra Base Hits In One Game.......................................87
Two Orioles Who Hit Two Doubles In One Inning..87
Two Orioles Who Struck Out Twice In One Inning 87
Three Orioles Who Struck Out At Least Five Times In One Game 88
Four Orioles Struck Out By Texas Ranger Bobby Witt In The Second Inning
    On August 2, 1987 88
Two Oriole Pitchers Who Walked Twelve Batters In A Nine-Inning Game 88
Four No-Hit Bids Broken Up By Al Bumbry 88
Six Oriole Catchers Who Had To Fill In At First Base ....˜9
Five Orioles Who Appeared In Just One Game In The Majors ....
Thirteen Players Who Appeared In Only One Game As An Oriole ....
Six Orioles Who Stole Home Against A Once Or Future Oriole Catcher ....

Seven Orioles Who Stole Home More Than Once...91
Ten Major League Team Records Held (Or Tied) By The Orioles.................................91
Eleven American League Team Records Held (Or Tied) By The Orioles 92
Four Miscellaneous Oriole Major League Records 92
Seven *Other* Major League Records Held By Cal Ripken, Jr. 93
Two Orioles Who Hit For The Cycle 94
Two Future Orioles Who Hit For The Cycle In 1950 With The Detroit Tigers...................94
Two Future Orioles Outfielders Who Hit For The Cycle With The Cincinnati Reds
    (Exactly 30 Years And One Month Apart) 94
Two Future Orioles Outfielders Who Hit For The Cycle With The Boston Red Sox 94
Four 1998 Orioles (Players Or Coaches) Who Were In The Top Five In Career RBI
    For Players Active Through The 1996 Season 94
13 Major League Batting Records Held (Or Shared) By An Oriole 95
Seven ALCS Batting Records Held (Or Tied) By John Lowenstein................................96
Three ALCS Batting Records Held (Or Tied) By Pitcher Mike Cuellar.........................96
Four ALCS Batting Records Tied By Rafael Palmeiro 96
Four ALCS Batting Records Held By Brooks Robinson 96
Ten ALCS Shortstop Fielding Records Held (Or Tied) By Orioles...................................97
Eight ALCS Pitchers Fielding Records Held (Or Tied) By Orioles...................................97
Two ALCS Catching Records Shared By Rick Dempsey And Chris Hoiles.....................98
Three ALCS Second Base Fielding Records Set By Roberto Alomar In 1996....................98
Nine ALCS Third Base Fielding Records Held (Or Tied) By Orioles................................98
Eleven ALCS First Base Fielding Records Held (Or Tied) By Orioles.............................99
Six ALCS Second Base Fielding Records Held (Or Tied) By Bobby Grich........................99
Four Orioles Who Hit A Home Run In Their First World Series At Bat 100
One World Series Batting Record Held By Jim Palmer 100
The Guys-Who-At-One-Time-Played-Third-Base-After-Brooks-Retired Team
    (and Where They Normally Played) 100
Three Orioles Who Played In At Least Ten Games At All Four Infield Positions...........100
Four Orioles Who Played All Four Infield Positions And Played In One Game
    In The Outfield 101
The Spent-Their-Entire-Major-League-Career-In-An-Orioles-Uniform Team.................101
13 Orioles Who Played One Year In Japan..102
Twelve Orioles Who Played More Than One Year In Japan 103
Two Orioles Who Played For A Major League-Record Ten Different Teams....................103

Chapter 9 • Firsts & Lasts...**104**
The First Five Players To Make Their Major League Debut With The Orioles.................105
Orioles Who Made Their Major League Debut On The Same Day 105
Ten Players With The Most Opening Day Starts For The Orioles 106
The All Opening-Day Team 106
Eleven Different Players Who Started In Right Field For The Orioles On
    Opening Day 1954-1964..107
Eight Opening Day Starters Better Known At Other Positions...107
Two Oriole Players Who Started At The Most Different Positions On Opening Day......108
Some Oriole Firsts 108
Four Orioles Who Were The First from Their Country To Play In The Major Leagues...109
14 Well-Known Opposing Players Who Ended Their Careers With The Orioles.............109

Chapter 10 • Birth, Life & Death...*110*

The Most Common Oriole Birthdays...*111*
The Most Common Months For Oriole Birthdays...*111*
The All-Born-In-California Team...*111*
Eleven Pairs Of Orioles Born On The Same Date.......................................*112*
Two Orioles Born In The Same Hospital As The Author Of This Book............*112*
17 Orioles Who Made Their Major League Debut With A Team From The City
    Where They Were Born..*113*
Eleven Cities Where The Most Orioles Were Born.....................................*113*
Twelve States Where the Most Orioles Were Born......................................*114*
Six States Where One Oriole Was Born...*114*
Four States Where No Orioles Were Born..*114*
The Twelve Countries Where The Most Orioles Were Born.........................*115*
Five Countries Where Only One Oriole Was Born......................................*116*
20 Non-Natives Who Settled In The Baltimore Area After Playing For The Orioles.......*116*
The All Born (*Or Raised) In Maryland Team...*117*
Must Be Something In The Water...*118*
Five Orioles Born In Europe...*118*
Two Orioles Who Sang The National Anthem At A Major League Game.........*118*
Two Orioles Who Received Military Honors...*119*
Orioles Who Missed Playing Time To Serve In The National Guard
    During The 1968 Riots...*119*
Four Orioles' High School Hi-Jinx...*119*
13 Orioles' Collegiate Capers..*120*
Nineteen Orioles Who Had "Spirited" Post-Baseball Careers......................*120*
The Three Most Common Oriole Dates Of Demise.....................................*122*
Two Orioles Who Died In Plane Crashes..*122*
Nine Orioles Who Died In The Same Town In Which They Were Born............*122*
The All-Deceased Team...*123*
Six Dead Batteries (And The Years They Were With The O's)......................*123*

Chapter 11 • Families..*124*

Seven Oriole Families..*125*
Two Orioles With Famous Ancestors..*125*
33 Orioles With A Relative Who Played In The Major Leagues (But Not With
    The Orioles)...*126*
Three Orioles With A Football-Playing Relative...*127*
One Oriole With A Basketball-Playing Relative..*127*

Chapter 12 • Physical..*128*

The Ten Tallest Orioles...*129*
The 17 Shortest Orioles...*129*
The Nine Heaviest Orioles..*130*
The Four Lightest Orioles...*130*
The Eight Oldest Orioles To Appear In A Game...*130*
The Nine Youngest Orioles To Appear In A Game......................................*131*
The All Teen-Age Team...*132*
Seven Things That Andy Etchebarren And Frank Zupo Have In Common.......*132*

The All Eyeglass-Wearing Team 133
Two Orioles With Mustaches Who Led A Japanese League In RBI.......................134
The All-Moustache Team...134
The All-Switch-Hitting Team 135

Chapter 13 • Managers & Coaches 136

The Orioles-Who-Became-Big-League-Managers Team 137
Seven Oriole Managers Of The Year 138
Two Teams That Have Been Managed By More Former Orioles Than The O's Have.....138
Six Teams Never Managed By A Former Oriole Player...138
Seven Orioles Who Played First Base And Outfield For The O's And Later
    Managed In The Bigs 139
The All-Oriole-Coaches-Who-Were-Also-Oriole-Players Team 139
Twelve Orioles Coaches Who Never Played In The Majors..................................140
The Five States Where The Most Orioles Managers And Coaches Were Born 140
Three Orioles Managers Or Coaches Who Died In The Same Town In Which
    They Were Born 140

Chapter 14 • Trades & Drafts 141

Three Players Who Had Three Tours of Duty with the Orioles 142
28 Players Who Had Two Tours Of Duty With The Orioles 143
Seven Players Traded For Elrod Hendricks 145
Eight Interesting Trades..146
Twelve Oriole First-Round Draft Picks Who Made It With The O's (1965-97).................148
Four Oriole First-Round Draft Picks Who Never Played With The O's,
    But Played In The Majors With Other Teams..149
21 Orioles Who Were First Round Draft Picks For Other Teams 149
Two Orioles Who Were Number One Overall Picks For Other Teams 150
Eight First Round Draft Picks Who Were With The Orioles in 1995 150
Six Orioles Draft Picks Who Didn't Sign with the Orioles—At Least Not Right Away ..150
The All Lost-In-The-Expansion-Draft Team 151

Chapter 15 • Minor Leagues 152

Orioles Farm Teams 1954-1998 153
Eight Orioles Who Were International League MVPs With The Rochester Red Wings ..155
Ten Orioles Who Were International League Rookie Of The Year With The
    Rochester Red Wings...155
Five Orioles Who Were International League Most Valuable Pitcher With The
    Rochester Red Wings...156
Five Orioles Who Were International League Batting Leaders With The
    Rochester Red Wings...156
Seven Orioles Who Were International League Home Run Leaders With The
    Rochester Red Wings...156
Eleven Orioles Who Won Other Minor League Awards...157
Seven Orioles Who Were Voted Minor League Player Of The Year 157
Two Oriole Pitchers Who Led The Minor Leagues In Won-Lost Percentage 158
Four Orioles Who Led The Minor Leagues In Batting 158
25 Teams Named "Orioles" NOT From Baltimore 158
47 Maryland Minor League Teams 159

Chapter 16 • Other Teams 162

The Ones-That-Got-Away Team 163
Nine Future Orioles Who Made Their Major League Debut From April 15 To
  April 20, 1952...163
Three Who Made Their Major League Debut With The Orioles And Were
  Later All-Stars With The California Angels..163
Two Orioles In The Baseball Hall Of Fame Who Made Their Major League
  Debut On April 17, 1956..164
Orioles Who Made Their Major League Debut On The Same Day,
  For The Same Team, But Not The O's..164
Two Oriole DHs Named Tommy Who Wore Number 12 And Played For
  The 1969 Seattle Pilots..164
Three Orioles Who Pitched A Shutout In Their First Major League Start
  (Though Not As An Oriole)...165
Four Orioles Who Hit Home Runs From Both Sides Of The Plate In The
  Same Game (Though Not With The Orioles)..165
Three Orioles Whose Numbers Were Retired By Other Teams.........................165
The All-Made-Their-Major-League-Debut-With-The-Tigers Team 166
Eight Long-Time Orioles Who Ended Their Careers With Other Teams
  (And Their Post-Oriole Stats) 166
Highs And Lows With Oriole Catcher Joe Ginsberg.......................................167
The All-Made-Their-Major-League-Debut-With-The-Reds Team 167
Four Orioles Who Played At Least 500 Games At Third Base For The
  Cincinnati Reds..167
Seven Now Defunct Teams That Oriole George Brunet Pitched For 168
Three Orioles Who Were World Series MVPs For The New York Yankees.........168
The All-Played-For-The-Old-Washington-Senators (Who Moved To Minnesota
  In 1961) Team 169
The All-Played-For-The-New-Washington-Senators (Who Moved To Texas
  In 1972) Team 169
Eight Teams Where At Least 10% Of Oriole Players Have Played (Out Of A
  Total Of 633 Orioles From 1954 Through 1998) 170
Eight Teams Where At Least 20 Orioles Made Their Major League Debut.........170
Two World Championship Teams Since 1950 That Had No Former
  Or Future Orioles 170
The All-Made-Their-Major-League-Debut-With-The-Cardinals Team...............171
Six Former Or Future Orioles Who Played With The A's Against The O's
  In The 1971 ALCS..171
Six Former Or Future Orioles Who Played With The Angel's Against The O's
  In The 1979 ALCS..171
Six Former Or Future Oriole Pitchers Who Won Games Against The O's
  In The Post Season 172
Four Former Or Future Orioles To Homer Against The O's In The Post Season 172
The All-Made-Their-Major-League-Debut-With-The-Yankees Team..................172
Two Orioles Who Played For Both The New York Yankees And
  The New York Giants..173
Six Orioles Who Played For Both The New York Yankees And The New York Mets.......173
Two Orioles Who Played For Both the Boston Red Sox And the Boston Braves.............173

Ten Orioles Who Played For Both the Chicago White Sox And The Chicago Cubs.........*173*
One Oriole Who Played For Both The Philadelphia Phillies And
  The Philadelphia A's *174*
The All-Made-Their-Major-League-Debut-With-The-Phillies Team *174*
Some Non-Oriole Firsts *174*
Four Orioles Who Were All-Stars Before And After Their Stint With
  The Orioles, But Not During *175*
The All-Made-Their-Major-League-Debut-With-The-Red Sox Team........................*175*
Three Orioles Who Were All-Star Shortstops For The Boston Red Sox *176*
Six Orioles Who Were All-Star Pitchers For The Detroit Tigers *176*
Five Orioles Who Were All-Star Pitchers For The New York Yankees.....................*176*
Four Orioles Who Were All-Star Pitchers For The Chicago White Sox *176*
Five Orioles Who Were All-Star Outfielders For The Chicago White Sox *177*
Three Orioles Who Were All-Star Shortstops For The Chicago White Sox.................*177*
The All-Made-Their-Major-League-Debut-With-The-White Sox Team *177*
Nine Orioles Who Played For The 1952 World Champion New York Yankees *178*
Ten Orioles Who Played For The 1953 World Champion New York Yankees..................*178*
Eight Orioles Who Played For The 1972 World Champion Oakland Athletics *179*
Eight Orioles Who Played For The 1986 World Champion New York Mets *179*
The All-Played-For-The-New-York-Giants Team *180*
Five Orioles Who Had Great Post-Season Moments—for Other Teams.....................*180*
The All-Made-Their-Major-League-Debut-With-The-Indians Team.............................*181*
19 Orioles Who Won Major Awards For Other Teams...*182*
Nine Other Teams Named The Baltimore Orioles *183*
And 13 More Baltimore Baseball Teams *184*

Chapter 17 • The Alphabet Teams *185*
The A Team *186*
The All-B Team...*186*
The All-C Team *186*
The All-D Team *186*
The All-F Team...*187*
The All-G Team...*187*
The All-H Team...*187*
The All-J Team...*187*
The Special-K Team *188*
The All-L Team...*188*
The All-M Team...*188*
The All-P Team...*188*
The All-R Team...*189*
The All-S Team *189*
The All-T Team *189*
The All-W Team *189*

Chapter 18 • All-Time Roster & Index.................................*190*

Foreword

by Dan Rodricks, The Baltimore Sun & WMAR-TV

Turkey Joe Trabert's attic, like so much of his life, is divided between beer and baseball. You could look it up. You could follow him up to the third floor of his shingled manse on Batavia Avenue, in the Hamilton section of Baltimore—the poor man's Roland Park, Turkey calls it—and, at the top of the stairs, you stand at the great divide. To the right: shelves of beer cans and bottles from bygone Baltimore breweries—Gunther's, National, American, Hamm's. To the left: a vast library of baseball books, magazines, signage, photographs, memorabilia collected during years of scavenger-hunting through yard sales and flea markets.

But he doesn't merely collect things; William Randolph Hearst did that. Turkey Joe savors things. He acquires a fine, old baseball book for a quarter at a flea market—the only thing the man buys new is food—and he actually reads most of it before assigning it to a shelf. He gets a new set of old beer coasters and he examines each one before filing them away in an appropriate shoe box. This past year, he inventoried his stuff with the goal of a complete catalog of his holdings, which number in the thousands.

The result of his studies of baseball and beer, Joe will tell you, is a mind crammed with useless information.

But, of course, it's not useless.

It's not useless because Turkey Joe uses what he knows about baseball and beer—and just about everything else Baltimorean—to entertain and inform. He was, when I think about it, the first purveyor of infotainment I ever knew. He dispensed his knowledge across the bar he owned in Fells Point. He didn't serve peanuts, he served factoids.

Amazing, a man of his age and barroom experience with such a prodigious memory. He retains trivia like my Aunt Grace retains water.

He's a hard man to stump. You can ask him just about anything. Usually, he doesn't have to look it up, either.

Joe, who was the catcher of the 1954 Orioles? What beer company sponsored the old scoreboard at Memorial Stadium? When was the first All-Star game played in Baltimore? Who threw out the game ball? Who was the first native Baltimorean to play for the Orioles?

It's even better when Joe and I get together for a beer. Baseball Billie Jones might be there, too; he's been going to Orioles games and visiting barrooms with Joe for a couple of decades. We play a little happy hour game, mano a mano. A conversation might go like this:

Turkey Joe: Did you know Hack Wilson died in Baltimore?
Me: No. In fact, I barely know who Hack Wilson was.
Baseball Billie: Do you know what major league record he holds?
TJ: It's an incredible record that might never be broken.
Me: I give up.

TJ: Most RBI in a season.

BB: A hundred and seventy five.

Me: OK. But did you know that the first time money from the Brink's robbery showed up it was at an amusement arcade on East Baltimore Street?

TJ: Is that right? Did you know Hack Wilson worked as a bartender at a bar on East Baltimore Street?

Billie: Did you know there once was a Turkish bath on East Baltimore Street?

Me: Did you know the guy who played Gomez on the original Addams Family television show as born in Baltimore?

BB: John Astin, sure. He was married to Patty Duke.

TJ: Do you see that guy in the dark jacket at the bar? His nickname is Crash. Do you know why they call him that?

Me: No.

BB: He's the one who crashed his plane into Memorial Stadium after a Colts game.

TJ: Yeah. But don't bring that up.

BB: Do you know who won the game that day?

TJ: Do you know what the score was?

And so it goes like that, every time we get together.

Both Turkey and Baseball can outdo me at trivia. When I go to meet them, I have to go prepared. (The bit about the Brink's robbery, for instance, I came across that in the Sun library, while researching a column. Newspaper work takes you pretty deep into the factoid mine. While reading long-ago clips, you come across all kinds of interesting items about government, sports, celebrities, public institutions, history. Most of the factual flotsam does not stick. What does—such as the Brink's job revelation—makes for good barroom conversation later on, when drinking men try to out-trivialize one another.) This book, by Dave Pugh , gives me the edge I've long sought.

Not even Turkey Joe or Baseball Billie will see "the nine heaviest Orioles" coming. They'll never expect me to ask them to name the "all eyeglass-wearing team." Forget about it!

Not even Turkey Joe could come up with the five Orioles born in Europe. And Baseball Billie? I respect the guy, but there's no way he'll be able to name the "two Oriole DHs who wore No. 12 and played for the 1969 Seattle Pilots." My God, the 1969 Seattle Pilots!

Pugh is to be...what? Admired? Praised? Pitied?

This book is incredible. I thoroughly enjoyed it. I was awed by it. And yet, I find myself wondering: Has Dave Pugh been out much the last few years? Does he know who Monica Lewinsky is?

Still, I thank him for his toil. He has given me an edge over Turkey Joe in the trivia department—however short-lived that superiority might be. Once this books gets out there and starts showing up on flea market tables for a quarter, I'm dead. ⊘

A Fan's History of the Baltimore Orioles
by Linda Geeson

The modern Baltimore Orioles arrived in the Land of Pleasant Living on April 15, 1954. The former St. Louis Browns were paraded down 33rd Street to Memorial Stadium, still not completely finished but close enough for that first American League Opening Day. A capacity crowd of more than 52,000 saw Vice President Richard Nixon toss out the ceremonial first pitch. The O's won 3-1.

Dave Pugh was born in 1957 and I arrived in 1959, but we both feel like the whole history of the modern Orioles parallels our lives. Both of us have planned important events—weddings, vacations, jobs—around the Orioles. We still do. It's a habit we developed as kids.

While the rest of the country was reeling with the cultural revolution called the '60s, here's what we Oriole fans were doing: Singing along with "Pennant Fever" in 1964, when the O's made their first genuine challenge to the hated Yankees. Dancing on the Orioles' dugout when the team swept the Dodgers in 1966 to win their first World Championship. Gasping in shock when the Orioles fired Hank Bauer in favor of some guy named Weaver. Learning to love Weaver. Being a Junior Oriole. Worshipping Brooksie.

The early '70s were a blur of gold and green, dominated by Charlie Finley's Oakland As. Remember Jim Palmer vs. Catfish Hunter? Lots of gold around in those days, too little of it in the form of World Series trophies for the Orioles. Crowds dwindled to the diehards. Like us.

By 1979, Orioles fandom was defined by Section 34 and the Rowdies—Bill Hagy and the gang leading cheers as the team staged a series of come-from-behind wins in June that set the stage for a tremendous year and a new surge in fan support. There were many heroes in those days: the young and amazing Eddie Murray, Ken "put it in the bullpen" Singleton, Lee May, Flanny, Rick Dempsey. At the final regular season home game that year, Dempsey led the players on the field in a giant Section 34-style "O-R-I-O-L-E-S," the memory of which still puts a lump in my throat. So does the memory of Willie Stargell putting the Orioles Magic team away for good in Game 7 of the '79 Series.

The Orioles challenged and fell short again in 1980-82, with the 1981 season marred by baseball's first extended strike. In 1982, the Orioles took the pennant race down to the wire in an unforgettable four-game season-closing series at home against the Milwaukee Brewers. A guy named Cal Ripken, Jr. had made his debut that season and would be Rookie of the Year. Earl Weaver was retiring, and there was a definite air of wanting to win one last pennant for the little general. Lose any one of those last four games, and the Orioles knew they were done. So they won the first three, and forced the Brew Crew to a sudden death final. Then lost. But the emotion from that final series carried over into the 1983 season, when the Orioles finally won their first World Championship since 1970.

Much of the 1980s was frustrating for us O's fans. But at least we got to watch Cal and Eddie, whom we trusted would be together forever in orange and black. Even that dream was busted when Eddie departed at the end of the 1988 season. Dave and I met midway through the 1989 season (remember catcher Mickey Tettleton's secret weapon, Fruit Loops? Yeah, but remember Greg Olson's season-blowing wild pitch in SkyDome?). The Orioles let us down in '89, but Dave and I have been friends ever since. Why not?

The 1990s have been a rollercoaster for Orioles fans. The 1991 season and 38 years at Memorial Stadium ended with a beautifully staged post-game ceremony on a chilly October afternoon. The old concrete horseshoe was packed with fans as Brooks Robinson took the field and stood alone at third base, the "Field of Dreams" theme underscoring our emotions. Frank Robinson, Jim Palmer, Boog Powell, all the heroes of our youth soon stood before us. It was splendid.

Oriole Park at Camden Yards opened April 6, 1992 and is arguably the most celebrated and imitated civic monument since the Empire State Building. The original *Book of Baltimore Orioles Lists* made its debut the next year while the team and the city were polishing things up to host the 1993 All-Star festivities, including a home run hitting contest that gave the game's best sluggers a chance to swing for the warehouse.

Speaking of that warehouse, what Orioles fan will ever forget the changing of the giant numbers that hung there in late summer 1995, as all of baseball counted down with us to the day when Cal Ripken would finally surpass Lou Gehrig's consecutive games played streak? For two nights that September we celebrated our hometown hero as he matched and then passed Gehrig with the dignity and quiet charm we've come to expect from baseball's Iron Man.

In the waning days of the millennium, the 1983 World Championship seems like something from a long time ago in a galaxy far, far away. Will there ever be another, a flag for our beautiful new ballpark? In the hearts of Orioles baseball fans, hope springs eternal. ⏀

Four Things That Dave Pugh Wants You To Know About This Book

1. The lists contain statistics and information available through the end of the 1998 season.
2. Many of the lists (you'll know which ones) are subjective (and are always open to discussion). Some of the lists are silly.
3. Every player who appears on a "Team" in this book actually played that particular position at least once in an Oriole uniform.
4. Any comments, corrections, suggestions and discussions are welcome and should be directed to Dave Pugh in care of American Literary Press.

Ten People That Dave Pugh Would Like To Thank

1. Cami Colarossi, for her never-ending support, encouragement, tolerance and assistance on this project (again)
2. Linda Geeson, unindicted co-conspirator and unrelenting Orioles fanatic, for her unwavering support of this project
3. Mike Ricigliano, for getting it (and drawing it!)
4. Dan Rodricks, for getting it (and writing about it!)
5. Johnnye Bradley of American Literary Press, for getting it (and publishing it, again!)
6. Jim Sutton of Specialist Marketing International, for getting it (and promoting it!)
7. Jim Burger, for the picture I didn't use
8. John Knott (my usher, Sec. 80) for the list I didn't use
9. Steve Pape, for the dead batteries
10. James Bready, for writing about the Orioles and inspiring me to do the same

Seven Things About Dave Pugh

1. Lives with his wife, Cami, and their cat, Martha, in Arcadia in Baltimore (on the southern end of the poor man's Roland Park)
2. Owns Dave Pugh Design (Better Living Thru Graphic Design—Since 1986)
3. Plays guitar and sings with Bad Neighbors—classic rock (the kind you like!)
4. Was born in Harford Memorial Hospital
5. Saw his first Orioles game in 1962 (versus the Los Angeles Angels) at the age of five
6. Has no idea how many O's games he has attended
7. Has no idea how many lists he has made

13 Resources For This Book

1. The Baltimore Orioles Media Guides, Yearbooks, Programs and Scorecards
2. *The Home Team* by James Bready (1984)
3. *Total Baseball: The Official Encyclopedia of Major League Baseball* edited by John Thorn, Pete Palmer, Michael Gershman and David Petrusza (Viking, 1997)
4. *The Sports Encyclopedia: Baseball* edited by Davis S. Neft and Richard M. Cohen (St. Martin's Press, 1992)
5. *The Great All-Time Baseball Record Book* by Joseph L. Reichler (MacMillan Publishing Company, 1993)
6. *Great Baseball Feats, Facts, & Firsts* by David Nemac (Signet, 1997)
7. *The Sporting News Complete Baseball Record Book* (The Sporting News, 1998)
8. *Professional Baseball Franchises* by Peter Filichia (Facts On File, 1993)
9. *SABR Presents The Home Run Encyclopedia* edited by Bob McConnell and David Vincent (MacMillan Publishing Company, 1996)
10. *Birds On The Wing* by Gordon Beard (Doubleday & Company, Inc., 1967)
11. *The Baltimore Orioles* by Ted Patterson (Taylor Publishing Company, 1994)
12. *USA Today's Baseball Weekly*
13. Rochester Red Wings, Bowie Baysox, Frederick Keys and Delmarva Shorebirds Media Guides.

1 • NAMES

The Six Most Common Oriole First Names

1. John   32
2. Robert   30
3. Michael   27
4. James   24
5. David   23
6. William   16

The Seven Most Common Oriole Last Names

1. Smith   11
2. Johnson   9
3. Brown   7
4. Jones   6
5. Davis   5
6. Miller   5
7. Robinson   5

The Seven Most Common Oriole Middle Names

1. Lee   26
2. Edward   24
3. Joseph   17
4. Thomas   14
5. Allen   12
6. Michael   12
7. Anthony   11

The Seven Most Common Names That Orioles Go By

1. Mike   29
2. Bob   28 (includes 8 Bobby's)
3. Dave   24 (includes 3 David's and 1 Davey)
4. Jim   23 (includes 3 Jimmy's)
5. John   20 (includes 3 Johnny's)
6. Bill   16 (includes 10 Billy's)
7. Tom   16 (includes 3 Tommy's)

The Eight Players Whose Name They Go By And Last Name Are On The Lists Of Most Common Names

1. Mike Smith
2. Mike Johnson
3. Bob Johnson
4. Dave Johnson
5. Dave Johnson
6. Dave Johnson
7. John Miller
8. Bill Miller

Two Players Whose First, Middle and Last Names, As Well As The Names They Go By, Are On The Lists Of Most Common Names

1. Michael Anthony "Mike" Smith
2. David Allen "Davey" Johnson

The All-Bob Team

SP	Milacki
RP	Reynolds
C	Melvin
1B	Boyd
2B	Grich
SS	Johnson
3B	Kennedy
OF	Nieman
OF	Nelson
OF	Saverine
DH	Oliver

The All-David-Dave-Davey Team

SP	Dave McNally
RP	Dave Leonhard
C	Dave Skaggs
1B	David Segui
2B	Davey Johnson
SS	Aaron David Ledesma
3B	Dave Philley
OF	Dave May
OF	Dave Nicholson
OF	David Dellucci
DH	Dave Gallagher

Three Orioles With The Same First And Last Names

1. David Allen "Davey" Johnson   2B, 1965-72
2. David Charles "Dave" Johnson   P, 1974-75
3. David Wayne "Dave" Johnson   P, 1989-91

Six Orioles With Kooky Middle Names

1. Vernon Edgell Bickford
2. Paul L.D. Blair
3. James Ehrenfeld Brideweser
4. Drungo Larue Hazewood *(Drungo?)*
5. Leslie Ferdinand "Buster" Narum
6. Louis Mortimer Sleater

13 Orioles Better Known By Their Middle Names

1. Kenneth JERRY Adair
2. Hector Harold "HAL" Brown
3. James KEVIN Brown
4. Herman Thomas "TOMMY" Davis
5. John Rikard "RICK" Dempsey
6. Charles Sidney "SID" Fernandez
7. Marcus WAYNE Garland
8. Wallace LARRY Haney
9. Gordon William "BILLY" Hunter
10. Harold Patrick "PAT" Kelly
11. Jose DENNIS Martinez
12. Larry Benard "BEN" McDonald
13. James HOYT Wilhelm

Six Oriole "Berts"

1. GilBERT Coan
2. OdBERT Hamric
3. Grady EdgeBERT Hatton
4. DelBERT Rice
5. Brooks CalBERT Robinson
6. John AlBERT Schmitz

Five Orioles Who Shortened Their Names

1. Dick Kokos (Kokoszka)
2. Dave Koslo (Koslowski)
3. Eddie Lopat (Lopatynski)
4. Erv Palica (Pavliecivich)
4. Milt Pappas (Miltiades Stergios Papastedgios)

Seven First, Middle And Last Names

1. Howard	**Howard** (Howie) Fox
	Curtell (Curt) **Howard** Motton
	Bruce **Howard**
2. Lee	**Lee** Smith
	Arthur **Lee** Rhodes
	Mark **Lee**
3. Leonard	**Leonard** (Lenny) Webster
	Stuart (Stu) **Leonard** Miller
	Mark **Leonard**
4. Nelson	**Nelson** Briles
	Paul **Nelson** Kilgus
	Bob **Nelson**
5. Scott	**Scott** Erickson
	Jeffrey (Jeff) **Scott** Ballard
	Micky **Scott**
6. Stuart	**Stuart** (Stu) Miller
	George **Stuart** Brunet
	Marlin **Stuart**
7. Thomas	**Thomas** (Tom) Niedenfuer
	John (Rocky) **Thomas** Coppinger
	Valmy **Thomas**

Six Oriole Catchers Whose Last Names Begin And End With The Same Letter

1. Joe Ginsberg
2. Joe Nolan
3. John Orsino
4. Larry Sheets*
5. Dave Skaggs
6. Jeff Tackett

OF/DH Larry Sheets caught in six games for the Orioles in 1985.

Groups Of Players With The Same Last Name Who Played On The Same Team

1. Brooks & Eddie Robinson	1957
2. Brooks & Earl Robinson	1961-62, 1964
3. John & Stu Miller	1963, 1956-67
4. Bob & Davey Johnson	1965-67
5. Brooks & Frank Robinson	1966-71
6. Eddie & Tom Fisher	1967
7. Grant & Reggie Jackson	1976
8. Dennis & Tippy Martinez	1976-86
9. Lee & Rudy May	1976-77
10. Cal, Jr. & Bill Ripken	1987-92, 1996
11. Glenn & Storm Davis	1992
12. Lee, Lonnie & Mark Smith	1994
13. Lee, Lonnie & Dwight Smith	1994
14. Randy & Jimmy Myers	1996
15. Charlie & Willie Greene	1998

The Orioles-With-Girlie-Names Team

P	Nellie Briles
P	Connie Johnson
C	Nathaniel Beverly "Nate" Smith
1B	Ellie Hendricks
2B	Neil "Connie" Berry
SS	Ronald Lavern Hansen
3B	Larry Leslie Brown
OF	John Patsy "Tito" Francona
OF	Angie Dagres
OF	Brad Lynn Komminsk

Sounds The Same, Spelled Differently

1. Bob Bailor & Don Baylor
2. Sammy Stewart & Marlin Stuart
3. Gene Green & Charlie Greene

The All-Alliterative Team

P	Mike Mussina
P	Robin Roberts
RP	Sammy Stewart
C	Clint Courtney
1B	Bob Boyd
2B	Mark McLemore
SS	Chico Carrasquel
3B	Doug DeCinces
OF	Bobby Bonilla
OF	Lee Lacy
OF	Tony Tarasco

Five Orioles With Fishy Names

1. Paul "Dizzy" Trout
2. Chico Salmon
3. Harvey Haddix
4. Marlin Stuart
5. Kevin Bass

Three Birds With Birdie Names

1. Harry Byrd
2. Mike Parrott
3. Terry Crowley

Eleven Orioles With Job Names

1. Frank Baker
2. Steve Barber
3. Mike Cook
4. Ed Farmer
5. Billy Gardner (!)
6. Billy Hunter
7. Jim Marshall
8. Stu Miller
9. Dave Pope
10. Keith Shepherd
11. Earl Weaver

Three Orioles With Car Names

1. Dave Ford
2. Luis Mercedes
3. Dan Ford

Ten Orioles With Colorful Names

1. Dick Brown
2. Gene Green
3. Larry Brown
4. Ted Gray
5. Mark Brown
6. Lenny Green
7. Marty Brown
8. Bill Wight (!)
9. Hal Brown
10. Kevin Brown

Three Orioles With Christmas Names

1. Billy Klaus
2. Wayne Garland
3. Ken Rudolph

Four Orioles With "Spirited" Names

1. Johnny Schmitz
2. John Miller
3. Rich Bordi
4. Dave Vineyard

Too Bad Bob Watson Never Was An Oriole

1. Doyle Alexander
2. Dan Graham
3. Juan Bell

Five Orioles With Team Names

1. Kevin Brown   Cleveland or St. Louis
                     (they both moved to Baltimore!)
2. Tim Laker   Los Angeles
3. Marlin Stuart   Florida
4. Dave Philley   Philadelphia
5. Royle Stillman   Kansas City

15 Orioles Better Known By Their Nicknames

1. Alfonso CHICO Carrasquel
2. John ROCKY Coppinger
3. George STORM Davis
4. Walter HOOT Evers
5. John TITO Francona
6. Vincio CHICO Garcia
7. Alfonso KIKO Garcia
8. Dorrel WHITEY Herzog
9. Terry TITO Landrum
10. Carroll WHITEY Lockman
11. Reynaldo CHITO Martinez
12. Felix TIPPY Martinez
13. John BOOG Powell
14. Rutherford CHICO Salmon
15. William James B.J. Surhoff

Four Pairs Of Orioles With The Same Nicknames

1. Bob Turley & Bob Reynolds   "Bullet Bob"
2. Lenn Sakata & Harry Brecheen   "Cat"
3. Andy Etchebarren & Mark Corey   "Lurch"
4. Gary Roenicke & Mike Reinbach   "Rhino"

Three Orioles Nicknamed "Moose"

1. Walt Dropo
2. Randy Milligan
3. Mike Mussina

Seven Orioles With Nicknames Based On Their Physical Attributes

1. "Little Louie" Aparicio
2. Mark "The Blade" Belanger
3. Hal "Skinny" Brown
4. "Big Ben" McDonald
5. Floyd "Honey Bear" Rayford
6. Tim "Big Foot" Stoddard
7. Rick "The Red Baron" Sutcliffe

Ten Orioles With Animal Nicknames

1. Frank "Penguin" Bertaina
2. Harry "The Cat" Brecheen
3. Al "Bumble Bee" Bumbry
4. Rick "The Rooster" Burleson
5. Terry "The Crow" Crowley
6. Paul "Gorilla" Gilliford
7. Larry "Hawk" Harlow
8. Roger "Spider" Nelson
9. Gregg "Otter" Olson
10. John "Horse" Orsino

Three Orioles With Nicknames Based On Their Personalities

1. Paul "Motor Mouth" Blair
2. Jackie "Flakey" Brandt
3. "Disco Dan" Ford

Nine Before And After Names

1. Bobby Floyd Rayford
2. Roger Nelson Briles
3. Billy O'Dell Jones
4. Pat Kelly Paris
5. Bob Nelson Simmons
6. Mickey Scott Erickson
7. Mark Lee Smith
8. Phil Bradley Pennington
9. Bob Melvin Rosario

With Apologies To ESPN's Chris Berman

1. Fred "Jelly" Beene
2. Jim Busby "Berkeley"
3. Chico "On A" Carrasquel
4. Camilo Carreon "My Wayward Son"
5. Gil Coan "Head"
6. Todd Cruz "Missile"
7. Ike "Pick" Delock
8. Chuck "Pierce" Diering
9. Tom "Put Up Yer" Dukes
10. Dave Duncan "Donuts"
11. Hank "Aluminum" Foiles
12. Jim "French" Frey
13. Joe Gaines "Burgers"
14. "Mister" Gene Green
15. John "Ain't Mis Be" Habyan
16. Don "Robin" Hood
17. Stacy Jones "You'd Better Watch Your Speed"
18. Joe "It's Not The Saddle You Need, It's The" Orsulak
19. Kelly "We'll Always Have" Paris
20. Jim "Everybody Into The" Poole
21. Willie "The World Is Your" Royster
22. Larry "Satin" Sheets
23. Andy "Dick" Van Slyke & Ray "Mary Tyler" Moore
24. Hoyt "Kaiser" Wilhelm

Two Right-Handed Orioles Submariners Whose First Names are Dick And Last Names Start With "H"

1. Hall
2. Hyde

Three Orioles Who Should Have Been Marx Brothers

1. Walt Dropo
2. Jim Hutto
3. Frank "Noodles" Zupo

The First-Name-Ends-In-"O" Team

SP	Fernando Valenzuela
RP	Armando Benitez
C	Camilo Carreon
1B	Francisco Melendez
2B	Roberto Alomar
SS	Kiko Garcia
3B	Leo Gomez
OF	Drungo Hazewood
OF	Gino Cimoli
OF	Tito Francona
DH	Geronimo Berroa

Reserves

OF	Leo Burke
SS	Chico Carrasquel
P	Francisco de la Rosa
IF	Chico Fernandez
2B	Chico Garcia
IF	Rene "Gonzo" Gonzales
3B	Leo Hernandez
OF	Tito Landrum
OF	Chito Martinez
P	Orlando Pena
C	Sergio Robles
3B	Aurelio Rodriguez
P	Nerio Rodriguez
IF	Chico Salmon
C	Orlando Sanchez

Top Ten Oriole Fab Four Hits Plus One

1. Ayala Submarine
2. The Ballard Of John And Yoko
3. And Your Byrd Can Sing
4. Carey That Weight
5. I'm Down
6. You've Got To Hyde Your Love Away
7. A Hard Day's Knight
8. While My Guitar Gent Lee Weeps
9. Rocky Raccoon
10. Old Brown Schu
11. Tackett To Ride

Seven From Mick And Keith
(Not Tettleton And Moreland)

1. Brown Sugar
2. 19th Nervous Rick Down
3. Mon Key Man
4. Let's Spend The Knight Together
5. It's Oliver Now
6. Heart Of Stone
7. Time Is Zaun My Side

Four Beach Boys Of Summer

1. Barber Ann
2. Cal Ifornia Girls
3. Shut Down
4. Help Miranda

Ten Rock And Roll Orioles

1. Harry "Yard" Byrd
2. Tom "Amboy" Dukes
3. Bobby "Pink" Floyd
4. Jim "Lovin' Spoon" Fuller
5. Mike "Captain Beef" Hart
6. Don "Def" Leppert
7. Dave "Fleetwood" McNally
8. Lee "Aero" Smith
9. Jeff "Sly & The Family" Stone
10. Steve "Rolling" Stone

Ten All-Stars Of The Silver Screen

1. Storm "Bette" Davis
2. Billy "Ava" Gardner
3. Wayne "Judy" Garland
4. Larry "Jean" Harlow
5. Billy "Kim" Hunter
6. Pat "Grace" Kelly
7. Harold "Debbie" Reynolds
8. Dorn "Liz" Taylor
9. Johnny "Shirley" Temple
10. Shane "Lana" Turner

A Bobby Bo Nanza

1. Francisco "Pon" de la Rosa
2. Charlie "Lorne" Greene
3. Robin "Pernell" Roberts

Birdland Or TV Land

1. The Adventures of Aase & Harriet
2. Brady "Bunch" Anderson
3. David "I Love" Dellucci
4. Dick "Hee" Hall
5. "Gentle" Ben McDonald
6. Wally "Wild Wild" Westlake

Eight, Eight, Eight Names In One

GASTALLERMERCEDESTRADAGRESSEGIANDERSON

Seven Cereal Killers

1. Johnny "Quaker" Oates
2. Dan "Golden" Graham
3. Del "Cream of" Rice
4. Jackie "Raisin" Brandt (also known as "Flakey")
5. Connie "Crunch" Berry
6. Alan "General" Mills
7. Dick Kokos "Puffs"

My Fair (Or Foul) Lady

1. Alan "Henry" Wiggins
2. Calvin "Colonel" Pickering
3. Dick "Elizadoo" Littlefield

20 Fun Name Combinations

1. McCormick & Schilling *(spicy!)*
2. Pagan & Pope
3. Hall & Oates
4. Coggins & Mussina
5. Nichols & Schilling
6. Valentine & Hart
7. Martin & Lewis
8. Gentile & Harshman
9. Westlake & Northrup *(a southpaw?)*
10. Parent & Papa
11. Bob Nieman & Marcus Wayne Garland
12. (Generals) Bradley, Patton & Marshall
13. Knight & Dukes
14. Joe Frazier & Dempsey
15. Gomez & Adams
16. Farmer & Vineyard
17. McDonald & Farmer
18. Lewis & Clark
19. Locke & Key
20. Frey & Cook

Answer To Eight, Eight, Eight Names In One
(page 19)

1. Tom Gastall
2. George Staller
3. Cal Ermer
4. Luis Mercedes
5. Chuck Estrada
6. Angie Dagres
7. Chuck Essegian
8. Brady Anderson

The Nine Shortest Last Names

1. Billy Cox
2. Howie Fox
3. Jimmy Key
4. Charlie Lau
5. Mark Lee
6. Dave May
7. Lee May
8. Rudy May
9. Esteban Yan

The Seven Longest Last Names

1. Arnie Portocarrero (12 letters)
2. Andy Etchebarren (11 letters)
3. Scott Kamieniecki (11 letters)
4. Scott Klingenbeck (11 letters)
5. Dick Littlefield (11 letters)
6. Marv Throneberry (11 letters)
7. Craig Worthington (11 letters)

The Only Three Players Named John To Ever Play Second Base For The Orioles

1. Outfielder John Lowenstein   1 game in 1983
2. Outfielder John Shelby   1 game in 1985
3. Catcher John Stefero   1 game in 1986

The Only Three Players Named Jeff To Ever Play Second Base For The Orioles Who Also Happen To Be The Only Three Players Named Jeff To Ever Play Shortstop For The Orioles

1. Jeff McKnight
2. Jeff Huson
3. Jeff Reboulet

The Most-Popular-Name-For-Each-Position Team

SP	Mike (12)
RP	Mike (29)
C	Dave (5)
1B	Bob (7)
2B	Billy (6)
SS	Billy (6)
3B	Billy (6)
OF	Jim (9)
OF	Bob (7)
OF	Mike (6)
DH	Bob, Jeff, Jim & Mike (4)

Five Billy's Who Played Second Base, Shortstop And Third Base For The Orioles

1. Cox
2. Gardner
3. Goodman
4. Klaus
5. Smith

Note: Billy Ripken was prevented from joining this list by his big brother.

The All-Presidents Team

RHP	Roric Harrison
LHP	Grant Jackson *(first and last name)*
C	Terry Kennedy
1B	Bob Johnson
2B	Davey Johnson
SS	Ron Washington
3B	Bobby Adams
OF	Dan Ford
OF	Stan Jefferson
OF	Donell Nixon
DH	Joe Carter

Reserves

P	Dave Ford
P	Bob Harrison
OF	Lou Jackson
OF	Reggie Jackson
3B	Ron Jackson
P	Jesse Jefferson
P	Connie Johnson
C	Darrell Johnson
P	Dave Johnson
P	David Johnson
P	Don Johnson
P	Ernie Johnson
P	Mike Johnson
3B	Bob Kennedy
P	Dorn Taylor
OF	Joe Taylor
P	Jim Wilson

Mike Ricigliano's Ten Favorite Orioles To Draw

1. Peter Angelos
2. Cal Ripken, Sr.
3. Eddie Murray
4. Earl Weaver
5. Jim Traber
6. Gregg Olson
7. The Orioles Bird
8. Albert Belle
9. Sid Fernandez
10. Johnny Oates

2 • NUMBERS

The Twelve Most Used Numbers

1. Number 21	29	Orioles
2. Number 6	24	
3. Number 27	24	
4. Number 37	24	
5. Number 2	23	
6. Number 24	23	
7. Number 17	22	
8. Number 30	22	
9. Number 36	22	
10. Number 14	21	
11. Number 34	21	
12. Number 35	21	

Five *Other* Orioles Who Wore Number 5

1. Bobby Young	1954-1955
2. Hank Majeski	1955
3. Angie Dagres	1955
4. Bobby Adams	1956
5. Grady Hatton	1956

Six Numbers Worn By Only One Oriole

1. Number 61	Dennis Martinez
2. Number 62	Rick Krivda
3. Number 63	Nerio Rodriguez
4. Number 66	Paul Kilgus
5. Number 75	Alan Mills
6. Number 77	Joe Borowski

The All-Number-17 Team

Coach Dick Bosman
P   Wayne Garland
C   Joe Nolan
1B   Walt Dropo
2B   Rick Burleson
SS   Chico Carrasquel
3B   Chris Sabo
OF   B. J. Surhoff
OF   Kevin Bass
OF   Leo Burke
DH   Pete Stanicek

Reserves
P   Mike Adamson
OF   Hoot Evers
P   Ed Farmer
OF   Jim Fridley
P   Pete Harnisch
P   Art Houtteman
P   John Miller
3B   Tom O'Malley
P   Arnie Portocarrero
P   Ken Rowe
P   Bill Wight

Two Orioles Who Wore Three Different Numbers During One Season

1. Ray Murray   Numbers 8, 9 and 14 in 1954
2. Angie Dagres   Numbers 34, 5 and 20 in 1955

17 Players Who Wore The Same Number For Ten Seasons Or More

	Seasons	*Number*
1. Brooks Robinson	21	5
2. Jim Palmer	19	22
3. Cal Ripken, Jr.	18	8
4. Mark Belanger	16	7
5. Mike Flanagan	15	46
6. Al Bumbry	13	1
7. Dave McNally	13	19
8. Paul Blair	12	6
9. Rick Dempsey	12	24
10. Andy Etchebarren	12	8
11. Eddie Murray	12	33
12. Boog Powell	12	26
13. Tippy Martinez	11	23
14. Scott McGregor	11	16
15. Brady Anderson	10	9
16. Dennis Martinez	10	30
17. Ken Singleton	10	29

Seven Non-Players Who Wore The Same Number For Ten Seasons Or More

	Seasons	*Number*
1. Elrod Hendricks	21	44
2. Earl Weaver	17	4
3. Harry Brecheen	14	31
4. Billy Hunter	14	55
5. George Bamberger	10	31
6. Jim Frey	10	41
7. Cal Ripken, Sr.	10	47

The Seven Orioles Who Wore
The Most Different Numbers

1. Chris Hoiles   5   Number 11 in 1989
                             Number 17 in 1989
                             Number 42 in 1990
                             Number 28 in 1990
                             Number 23 from 1991-

2. Jerry Adair   4   Number 6 in 1958
                             Number 20 from 1958-59
                             Number 8 in 1959
                             Number 7 from 1959-66

3. Don Ferrarese   4   Number 20 in 1955
                             Number 21 from 1955-56
                             Number 39 in 1956
                             Number 32 in 1957

4. Bob Hale	4	Number 6 in 1955, 1956, 1957
		Number 34 from 1955-56
		Number 20 in 1958
		Number 10 in 1959
5. Billy O'Dell	4	Number 24 in 1954
		Number 18 in 1956
		Number 38 from 1957-1958
		Number 41 from 1958-1959
6. Mark Parent	4	Number 27 in 1992
		Number 6 in 1993
		Number 13 in 1993
		Number 24 in 1996
7. Brooks Robinson	4	Number 34 in 1955
		Number 21 in 1955
		Number 6 from 1956-1957
		Number 5 from 1957-1977

13 Orioles Who Wore Lucky Number 13

1. Charlie Locke	1955
2. Bill Miller	1955
3. Steve Barber	1961-1967
4. Roger Freed	1970
5. Doyle Alexander	1972-1976
6. Odell Jones	1986
7. Rick Schu	1988-1989
8. Dan Boone	1990
9. Mark Parent	1993
10. Mike Pagliarulo	1993
11. Don Buford	1994 (as a coach)
12. Andy Etchebarren	1996-97 (as a coach)
13. Ozzie Guillen	1998

The Only Five Numbers Worn By
Orioles Pitching Coaches

1. Number 31	Harry Brecheen from 1954-67
	George Bamberger from 1968-77
	Ray Miller from 1978-85 & 1997
	Ken Rowe in 1986
	Mark Wiley in 1987
	Herm Starrette in 1988
	Al Jackson from 1989-91
2. Number 42	Ken Rowe in 1985
3. Number 17	Dick Bosman in 1992-95
4. Number 46	Mike Flanagan in 1995 & 1998
5. Number 37	Pat Dobson in 1996

Two Orioles Who Wore Two Different
Numbers While With The Orioles,
Yet Appeared In Just One Game

1. Ryne Duren	Numbers 36 and 26 in 1954
2. Gordie Sundin	Numbers 24 and 27 in 1956

The Five Uniform Numbers
Retired By The Orioles

1. Number 20	Frank Robinson
2. Number 5	Brooks Robinson
3. Number 4	Earl Weaver
4. Number 22	Jim Palmer
5. Number 33	Eddie Murray

The Last Five Players To Wear The Retired Numbers Before The Retirees Did

1. Dave Vineyard   Number 20 in 1964
2. Grady Hatton   Number 5 in 1956
3. Mike Epstein   Number 4 in 1967
4. Dean Stone   Number 22 in 1963
5. Jim Hutto   Number 33 in 1975

Two Orioles Who Wore *Two* Numbers That Were Eventually Retired

1. Angie Dagres   Number 5 and Number 20 in 1955
2. Dave Philley   Number 4 in 1955-56
                     Number 22 in 1960-61

Seven Oriole Catchers Who Wore Number 10

1. Dick Brown
2. Clint Courtney
3. Tom Gastall
4. Elrod Hendricks
5. Les Moss
6. Tom Patton
7. Sergio Robles

Three Orioles Who Wore Number 15 And Later Managed In The Bigs

1. Davey Johnson
2. Eddie Lopat
3. Sam Mele

Three Orioles Who Wore Number 25 And Later Managed In The Bigs

1. Don Baylor
2. Whitey Lockman
3. Ray Knight

Same Last Name, Same Number

1. Hal and Marty Brown	Number 28
2. Larry and Mark Brown	Number 21
3. Joe and Rip Coleman	Number 35
4. Connie and Darrell Johnson	Number 36
5. Stu and Dyar Miller	Number 37
6. John and Randy Miller	Number 35
7. Cal, Sr. and Bill Ripken	Number 7
8. Brooks, Earl and Jeff Robinson	Number 34
9. Nate and Lonnie Smith	Number 27
10. Roy and Mark Smith	Number 14
11. Earl and Garrett Stephenson	Number 52

The All Prime Number Team

RHP	Doyle Alexander	Number 13
LHP	Billy O'Dell	Number 41
RP	Tippy Martinez	Number 23
C	Gus Triandos	Number 11
1B	Glenn Davis	Number 37
2B	Bobby Grich	Number 3
SS	Mark Belanger	Number 7
3B	Brooks Robinson	Number 5
OF	Al Bumbry	Number 1
OF	Al Pilarcik	Number 2
OF	Fred Lynn	Number 19
DH	Ken Singleton	Number 29

Two Maryland-Born Oriole Shortstops Who Wore Number 8

1. Tim Nordbrook   1975-76
2. Cal Ripken, Jr.   1981-

Ten Oriole-Magic Things About The Number 268

1. Joe Ginsberg's on-base percentage in 1959 (.268)
2. Mark Belanger's at-bats during the 1980 season
3. Luis Mercedes' birth month and year (2/68)
4. Jim Palmer's team-leading ERA in 1971 (2.68)
5. Opponents batting average versus Craig Lefferts in his five games as an Oriole in 1992 (.268)
6. Davey Johnson's total extra-base hits as an Oriole
7. Bob Johnson's slugging average in 1966 (.268)
8. Frank Robinson's 1968 batting average (.268)
9. Jim Palmer's career win total
10. Brooks Robinson's career home run total

Ten Numbers Worn By Three Orioles In The Same Season In The 1950s

1. #5 in 1955	Bobby Young, Hank Majeski & Angie Dagres
2. #6 in 1957	Bob Hale, Brooks Robinson & Art Houtteman
3. #14 in 1955	Wally Westlake, Gene Woodling & Jim Dyck
4. #15 in 1954	Sam Mele, Frank Kellert & Bob Kuzava
5. #20 in 1955	Art Schallock, Don Ferrarese & Angie Dagres
6. #21 in 1955	Brooks Robinson, Gil Coan & Don Ferrarese
6. #21 in 1957	Art Houtteman, Sandy Consuegra & Lenny Green
7. #23 in 1957	Dick Williams, Milt Pappas & Jim Busby
8. #24 in 1954	Joe Durham, Vern Bickford & Billy O'Dell
9. #25 in 1955	Bob Harrison, Jim McDonald & Ted Gray
10. #27 in 1956	Fred Besana, Gordie Sundin & Charlie Beamon
10. #27 in 1959	Joe Taylor, Wes Stock & Fred Valentine

Four Orioles Who Wore Number 34 During The 1955 Season

1. Brooks Robinson
2. Charlie Maxwell
3. Angie Dagres
4. Bob Hale

Five Numbers Worn By Three Orioles In The Same Season Since The 1950s

1. #6 in 1993   Harold Reynolds, Mark Parent & Mike Pagliarulo
2. #21 in 1990   Donell Nixon, Anthony Telford & David Segui
3. #29 in 1995   Brad Pennington, Gene Harris & Cesar Devarez
4. #30 in 1986   Dennis Martinez, Ricky Jones & Kelly Paris
5. #32 in 1998   Bobby Munoz, Jesus Tavarez & Lyle Mouton

The Identical-Double-Digit Team

SP	Jim Palmer	#22
RP	Paul Kilgus	#66
C	Gus Triandos	#11
1B	Eddie Murray	#33
2B	Rich Dauer	#44
SS	Luis Aparicio	#11
3B	Doug DeCinces	#11
OF	Dave Philley	#22
OF	Willie Tasby	#44
OF	Pete Incaviglia	#55
DH	Terry Crowley	#11

3 • HOME RUNS

Six Orioles Who Hit Three Consecutive Home Runs In A Game

1. Boog Powell	August 10, 1963
2. Bobby Grich	June 18, 1974
3. Don Baylor	July 2, 1975
4. Eddie Murray	August 29, 1979
5. Randy Milligan	June 9, 1990
6. Roberto Alomar	April 26, 1997

Seven Orioles Who Hit Three Non-Consecutive Home Runs In A Game

1. Boog Powell	June 27, 1964
	August 15, 1966
2. Curt Blefary	June 6, 1967
3. Paul Blair	April 29, 1970
4. Eddie Murray	September 14, 1980
	August 26, 1985
5. Dan Ford	July 20, 1983
6. Lee Lacy	June 8, 1986
7. Cal Ripken, Jr.	May 28, 1996

Two Games In Which The Orioles Hit Four Home Runs In One Inning

1. May 17, 1967 7th inning	Andy Etchebarren Sam Bowens Boog Powell Davey Johnson
2. September 5, 1995, 2nd inning	Chris Hoiles Jeff Manto Mark Smith Brady Anderson

Six Games In Which The Orioles Hit Three Consecutive Home Runs In One Inning

1. April 30, 1961   Jim Gentile
   7th inning   Gus Triandos
                           Ron Hansen
2. September 10, 1965   Brooks Robinson
   8th inning   Curt Blefary
                           Jerry Adair
3. September 4, 1969   Frank Robinson
   9th inning   Boog Powell
                           Brooks Robinson
4. May 8, 1979   Eddie Murray
   6th inning   Lee May
                           Gary Roenicke
5. September 16, 1985   Cal Ripken, Jr.
   8th inning   Eddie Murray
                           Fred Lynn
6. September 5, 1995   Jeff Manto
   2nd inning   Mark Smith
                           Brady Anderson

Three Former Oriole Pitchers Who Gave Up Eddie Murray's First Three Career Home Runs

1. Pat Dobson   April 18, 1977 with the Indians
2. Don Hood   April 20, 1977 with the Indians
3. Ken Holtzman   April 26, 1977 with the Yankees

Two Oriole Pitchers Who Gave Up Three Home Runs To Eddie Murray

1. Doyle Alexander (while with the Blue Jays and Tigers)
2. Sid Fernandez (while with the Mets and the Orioles)

Three Oriole Pitchers Who Gave Up Home Runs To Roger Maris In 1961

1. Chuck Estrada   #7 on May 21
2. Milt Pappas   #59 on September 20
3. Jack Fisher   #60 on September 26

Six Orioles Who Hit A Home Run In Their First Major League At Bat (Though Not Necessarily With The Orioles)

1. Whitey Lockman   July 5, 1945 with the N.Y. Giants
2. Bob Nieman   September 14, 1951
   with the St. Louis Browns
3. Hoyt Wilhelm   April 23, 1952
   with the N.Y. Giants
4. Don Leppert   June 18, 1961 with the Pirates
5. Buster Narum   May 3, 1963 with the Orioles
6. Benny Ayala   August 27, 1974 with the Mets

Four Orioles Who Hit Home Runs From Both Sides Of The Plate In The Same Game

1. Don Buford   April 9, 1970
2. Eddie Murray   August 3, 1977
   August 29, 1979
   August 16, 1981
   April 24, 1982
   August 26, 1982
   August 26, 1985
   May 8, 1987
   May 9, 1987
3. Mike Young   August 13, 1985
4. Mickey Tettleton   June 13, 1988

Two Games In Which The Orioles Hit Back-To-Back Pinch-Hit Home Runs

1. August 26, 1966   Vic Roznovsky and Boog Powell
9th inning off of Boston's
Lee Stange
2. August 12, 1985   Wayne Gross and Larry Sheets
9th inning off of Cleveland's
Jerry Reed

Two Games In Which The Orioles' First Two Batters Hit Home Runs

1. June 23, 1988   Ken Gerhart and Fred Lynn
off of Toronto's Jim Clancy
2. July 8, 1992   Brady Anderson and Mike
Devereaux off of Minnesota's
Scott Erickson

Two Innings In Which Both Cal And Bill Ripken Homered

1. 5th inning, September 15, 1990 versus Toronto
(off of future Oriole David Wells)
2. 9th inning, May 28, 1996 versus Seattle

Four Orioles To Hit 20 Home Runs And Steal 20 Bases In A Season

1. Paul Blair   26 HR & 20 SB in 1969
2. Don Baylor   25 HR & 32 SB in 1975
3. Reggie Jackson   27 HR & 28 SB in 1976
4. Brady Anderson   21 HR & 53 SB in 1992
                     50 HR & 21 SB in 1996

Two Famous Home Runs Given Up By Oriole Pitchers

1. Ted Williams' 521st and final home run given up by Jack Fisher
2. Micky Mantle's 500th surrendered by Stu Miller

Four Orioles Who Hit Home Runs In The Seventh Inning On May 17, 1967

1. Andy Etchebarren
2. Sam Bowens
3. Boog Powell
4. Davey Johnson

Note: Paul Blair, Brooks Robinson and Frank Robinson also hit home runs in this game.

Eight Oriole Home Run Events That Happened On August 26th

1. 1966   Vic Roznovsky and Boog Powell hit back-to-back pinch-hit home runs
2. 1968   Dave McNally hits a grand slam home run
3. 1973   Paul Blair hits a grand slam home run
4. 1979   Doug DeCinces hits a grand slam home run
5. 1982   Eddie Murray homers from both sides of the plate; one home run is a grand slam
6. 1985   Eddie Murray homers from both sides of the plate; one home run is a grand slam; Murray hits a total of 3 home runs and has 9 RBI; John Shelby, Floyd Rayford, Gary Roenicke and Rick Dempsey also homer.
7. 1996   Chris Hoiles hits a grand slam home run
8. 1997   Brady Anderson hits a grand slam home run

Six Orioles Who Hit Grand Slams On August 26th

1. Dave McNally   1968
2. Bob Grich   1973
3. Doug DeCinces   1979
4. Eddie Murray   1982 and 1985
5. Chris Hoiles   1996
6. Brady Anderson   1997

Most Popular Days Of The Month For Orioles Grand Slams

1. the 26th   15 grand slams
2. the 6th   12 grand slams
3. the 5th   9 grand slams
4. the 13th   9 grand slams
5. the 21st   9 grand slams

Least Popular Day Of The Month For Orioles Grand Slams

1. the 11th   1 grand slam

The Orioles have hit at least one grand slam on every day of the month.

Six Days When Two Oriole Grand Slams Were Hit

1. April 24, 1960   Billy Klaus and Albie Pearson
2. May 9, 1961   Jim Gentile
3. June 26, 1970   Frank Robinson
4. August 14, 1976   Reggie Jackson and Lee May
5. August 6, 1986*   Jim Dwyer and Larry Sheets
6. August 14, 1998   Chris Hoiles

* Same inning (The Rangers' Toby Harrah also hit a grand slam in this game.)

Three Times Oriole Grand Slams Were Hit On Consecutive Days

1. July 23 and 24, 1979   Pat Kelly and
                             John Lowenstein
2. August 15 and 16, 1981   Doug DeCinces and
                             Eddie Murray
3. August 26 and 27, 1997   Brady Anderson and
                             Rafael Palmeiro

Eleven Orioles Who Hit Pinch-Hit Grand Slams

1. Jim Gentile	1961	
2. Pat Kelly	1979 & 1980	
3. Benny Ayala	1982	
4. Dan Ford	1982	
5. Terry Crowley	1982	
6. John Lowenstein	1983	
7. Ken Singleton	1984	
8. Phil Bradley	1990	
9. Sam Horn	1990	
10. Joe Orsulak	1991	
11. Dwight Evans	1991	

Half of the 32 pinch-hit grand slams hit in the American League between 1980 and 1992 were hit by players who at one time played for the Orioles.

Seven Orioles Who Are All-Time Home Run Leaders For Their Home State

1. Brooks Robinson	Arkansas
2. Dave May (tie)	Delaware
3. John Lowenstein	Montana (Dave McNally is #3)
4. Jackie Brandt	Nebraska (Ron Hansen is #2)
5. Reggie Jackson	Pennsylvania
6. Frank Robinson	Texas (Don Baylor is #5)
7. Mike Devereaux	Wyoming

Cal Ripken, Jr. and Harold Baines rank #4 and #5 behind Babe Ruth, Jimmie Foxx and Al Kaline from Maryland.

Six Orioles Who Are Second On The All-Time Home Run List For Their Home State

1. Eddie Murray   California (behind Ted Williams)
2. Boog Powell   Florida (behind Andre Dawson)
3. Lenn Sakata   Hawaii (behind Mike Lum)
4. Fred Lynn   Illinois (behind Greg Luzinski)
5. Ron Hansen   Nebraska (behind Jackie Brandt)
6. Vern Stephens   New Mexico (behind Ralph Kiner)

Three Orioles In The Top Five All-Time Home Run Leaders Whose Last Name Begins With The Letter "R"

1. Frank Robinson   #2
2. Cal Ripken, Jr.   #4
3. Brooks Robinson   #5

Babe Ruth is #1; Jim Rice is #3.

24 Orioles Pitchers Who Hit Regular Season Home Runs

1. Dave McNally	9 *(includes one grand slam)*
2. Milt Pappas	9
3. Jack Harshman	7 *(six in 1958, including two in one game twice)*
4. Steve Barber	5
5. Mike Cuellar	5
6. Ray Moore	5
7. Jim Palmer	3
8. Eddie Watt	3
9. Jim Hardin	2
10. Billy O'Dell	2
11. Tom Phoebus	2

12. Gene Brabender   1
13. Joe Coleman   1
14. Chuck Estrada   1
15. Jack Fisher   1
16. Dick Hall   1
17. Roric Harrison   1
18. Bruce Howard   1
19. Grant Jackson   1
20. Don Larsen   1
21. Mike McCormick   1
22. Arnie Portocarrero   1
23. Jerry Walker   1
24. Buster Narum   1 *(first major league at bat & only plate appearance as an Oriole)*

Four Oriole Pitchers Who Hit Two Home Runs In One Game With Either The Tigers Or The Orioles

1. Babe Birrer   July 19, 1955 with the Tigers
2. Billy Hoeft   July 14, 1957 with the Tigers
3. Jack Harshman   July 16, 1958 with the Orioles
    September 23, 1958 with the O's
4. Milt Pappas   August 27, 1961 with the Orioles

Two Oriole Pitchers Who Hit Post-Season Home Runs

1. Dave McNally   2
    Game 5 of 1969 ALCS
    Game 3 of 1970 World Series (Grand Slam)
2. Mike Cuellar   1
    Game 1 of 1969 ALCS (Grand Slam)

4 • PITCHERS & PITCHING

Twelve Orioles Team Pitching Triple Crown Winners
(led team in wins, strikeouts & ERA)

1. Jim Palmer	1972, 1973, 1975, 1976, 1977
2. Mike Boddicker	1984, 1987 (tied for wins with Bell & Schmidt)
3. Steve Barber	1963
4. Mike Flanagan	1979
5. Connie Johnson	1957
6. Dave McNally	1968
7. Bob Milacki	1991
8. Mike Mussina	1994, 1995, 1996
9. Tom Phoebus	1967
10. Steve Stone	1980
11. Hoyt Wilhelm	1959 (tied with Pappas for wins)
12. Jim Wilson	1955

Five Oriole No-Hitters

1. Hoyt Wilhelm	9/20/1958 vs. Yankees
2. Steve Barber & Stu Miller	4/30/67 vs. Tigers (O's lost 2-1)
3. Tom Phoebus	4/27/68 vs. Red Sox
4. Jim Palmer	8/13/69 vs. A's
5. Bob Milacki, Mike Flanagan, Mark Williamson & Gregg Olson	7/13/91 vs. A's

Two Orioles No-Hitters Spoiled In The Ninth Inning By The Twins Cesar Tovar In 1969

1. May 15, with one out versus Dave McNally
2. August 10, with no outs versus Mike Cuellar

Eleven Oriole 20-Game Winners

1. Steve Barber	20 wins in 1963
2. Dave McNally	22 wins in 1968
	20 wins in 1969
	24 wins in 1970
	21 wins in 1971
3. Mike Cuellar	23 wins in 1969
	24 wins in 1970
	20 wins in 1971
	22 wins in 1974
4. Jim Palmer	20 wins in 1970
	20 wins in 1971
	21 wins in 1972
	22 wins in 1973
	23 wins in 1975
	22 wins in 1976
	20 wins in 1977
	21 wins in 1978
5. Pat Dobson	20 wins in 1971
6. Mike Torrez	20 wins in 1975
7. Wayne Garland	20 wins in 1976
8. Mike Flanagan	23 wins in 1979
9. Steve Stone	25 wins in 1980
10. Scott McGregor	20 wins in 1980
11. Mike Boddicker	20 wins in 1984

Five Great Pitchers Who Lost
At Least 20 Games To The Orioles

	Losses	*Career* *Won-Lost Pct.*
1. Jim "Catfish" Hunter	24	.574
2. Luis Tiant	22	.571
3. Jim Perry	22	.563
4. Fritz Peterson	21	.504
5. Jim Kaat	21	.544

Six Oriole Pitchers With Impressive
Single-Season Winning Streaks

1. Dave McNally	15 games in 1969
	13 games in 1971
	12 games in 1968
2. Steve Stone	14 games in 1980
3. Rick Sutcliffe	14 games in 1984 (with the Cubs)
4. Scott Erickson	13 games in 1991 (with the Twins)
	12 games in 1991 (with the Twins)
5. Phil Regan	13 games in 1966 (with the Dodgers)
6. Pat Dobson	12 games in 1971

Four Orioles Pitchers To Go Undefeated In
A Season (With At Least Five Wins)

1. Grant Jackson	8-0 in 1973
2. Wes Stock	7-0 in 1963
	5-0 in 1961
3. Moe Drabowsky	6-0 in 1966
4. Jay Tibbs	5-0 in 1989

Four Orioles Who Pitched A Shutout In Their First Major League Start

1. Charlie Beamon   September 26, 1956
2. Dave McNally   September 26, 1962
3. Tom Phoebus   September 15, 1966
4. Ben McDonald   July 21, 1990

Tom Phoebus also pitched a shutout in his second major league start on September 20, 1966.

Four California Angels Struck Out By Mike Cuellar In The Fourth Inning On May 29, 1970

1. Alex Johnson
2. Ken McMullen
3. Tommie Reynolds
4. Jim Spencer

Five Non-Pitchers Who Pitched For The Orioles

1. Manny Alexander (2B) – 1996
   1 G, 0² IP, 0 W, 0 L, 0 SO, 4 BB, 1 H, 1 HR, 67.50 ERA
2. Todd Cruz (3B) – 1984
   1 G, 1 IP, 0 W, 0 L, 0 SO, 0 BB, 0 H, 0 HR, 0.00 ERA
3. Larry Harlow (OF) – 1978
   1 G, 0² IP, 0 W, 0 L, 1 SO, 4 BB, 2 H, 1 HR, 67.50 ERA
4. Elrod Hendricks (C) – 1978
   1 G, 2¹ IP, 0 W, 0 L, 0 SO, 1 BB, 1 H, 0 HR, 0.00 ERA
5. Jeff Tackett (C) – 1993
   1 G, 1 IP, 0 W, 0 L, 0 SO, 1 BB, 1 H, 0 HR, 0.00 ERA

Three Major League Pitching Records Shared By An Oriole

1. Most Consecutive Games Won By A Reliever In Three Consecutive Games – 3, Grant Jackson, 9/29/74 thru 10/1/74
2. Most Wins In One Day – 2, Wes Stock, 5/26/63
3. Most Losses In One Day – 2, Don Aase, 8/28/86

Five Oriole Pitchers Who Led The League In Shutouts

1. Steve Barber	8 in 1961
2. Mike Boddicker	5 in 1983
3. Mike Flanagan	5 in 1979
4. Mike Mussina	4 in 1995
5. Jim Palmer	5 in 1970 and 10 in 1975

Five Oriole Pitchers Who Led
The League With The Fewest Hits
Plus Walks Per Nine-Inning Game

1. Hal Brown	10.1 in 1960
2. Scott McGregor	9.8 in 1979
3. Dave McNally	7.9 in 1968
4. Mike Mussina	9.8 in 1992
5. Jim Palmer	10.4 in 1982

Seven Oriole Pitchers Who Led The
League In Won-Lost Percentage

1. Wally Bunker	.792 in 1964
2. Mike Cuellar	.750 in 1970 and .688 in 1974
3. Dave McNally	.808 in 1971
4. Mike Mussina	.783 in 1992
5. Jim Palmer	.800 in 1969 and .750 in 1982
6. Steve Stone	.781 in 1980
7. Mike Torrez	.690 in 1975

Four Oriole Pitchers Who Led The League
In Complete Games

1. Mike Cuellar	21 in 1970
2. Dennis Martinez	18 in 1979
3. Jim Palmer	22 in 1977
4. Scott Erickson	11 in 1998

Four Oriole Pitchers Who Led The League In Games Pitched

1. Eddie Fisher   67 in 1966
2. Stu Miller   71 in 1963
3. Jesse Orosco   65 in 1995
4. George Zuverink   62 in 1956 and 56 in 1957

Three Oriole Pitchers Who Led The League In Saves

1. Stu Miller   27 in 1963
2. Randy Myers   45 in 1997
3. Lee Smith   33 in 1994
4. George Zuverink   16 in 1956

Three Oriole Pitchers Who Led The League In Opponents Batting Average

1. Mike Boddicker   .216 in 1983
2. Chuck Estrada   .218 in 1960 and .207 in 1961
3. Bob Turley   .203 in 1954

Six Oriole Pitchers Who Led The League In Opponents On Base Percentage

1. Hal Brown   .286 in 1960
2. Mike Cuellar   .261 in 1969
3. Scott McGregor   .275 in 1979
4. Mike Mussina   .279 in 1992
5. Jim Palmer   .287 in 1982
6. Robin Roberts   .272 in 1963

Nine Oriole Pitchers Who Led The League (Or Tied For The League Lead) In Wins

1. Mike Boddicker	20 in 1984
2. Mike Cuellar	24 in 1970
3. Chuck Estrada	18 in 1960
4. Mike Flanagan	23 in 1979
5. Dennis Martinez	14 in 1981
6. Dave McNally	24 in 1970
7. Mike Mussina	19 in 1995
8. Jim Palmer	23 in 1975, 22 in 1976 and 20 in 1977
9. Steve Stone	25 in 1980

Three Oriole Pitchers Who Led The League In Earned Run Average

1. Mike Boddicker	2.79 in 1984
2. Jim Palmer	2.40 in 1973 and 2.09 in 1975
3. Hoyt Wilhelm	2.19 in 1959

Five Pitching Categories Led By Oriole Pitchers In 1970

1. Wins	Dave McNally (24) Mike Cuellar (24)
2. Won-Lost Percentage	Mike Cuellar (.750)
3. Complete Games	Mike Cuellar (21)
4. Shutouts	Jim Palmer (5)
5. Innings Pitched	Jim Palmer (305)

Six Pitching Categories Led By Oriole Pitchers In 1979

1. Wins   Mike Flanagan (23)
2. Complete Games   Dennis Martinez (18)
3. Shutouts   Mike Flanagan (5)
4. Innings Pitched   Dennis Martinez (292⅓)
5. Hits+Walks/9 Innings   Scott McGregor (9.8)
6. Opponents On Base %   Scott McGregor (.275)

Four A.L. Or Major League Pitching Categories Led By Scott Erickson In 1998

1. Games Started   36 (M.L.)
2. Complete Games   11 (A.L.)
3. Ground Outs   393 (M.L.)
4. Ground Out/
   Fly Out Ratio   2.65 (A.L.)

Eight Oriole Pitchers Who Hit Triples

1. Mike Adamson   1 in 1967
2. Hal Brown   2 (1 in 1957, 1 in 1959)
3. Mike Cuellar   1 in 1969
4. Chuck Estrada   1 in 1960
5. Jim Hardin   2 (1 in 1967, 1 in 1969)
6. Don Larsen   3 in 1954
7. Stu Miller   1 in 1963
8. Milt Pappas   1 in 1965

18 Switch-Hitting Pitchers

1. Fred Beene
2. Mark Brown
3. Art Ceccarelli
4. Jim Dedrick
5. Francisco de la Rosa
6. Ken Dixon
7. Ted Gray
8. Pete Harnisch
9. Bruce Howard
10. Grant Jackson
11. Bob Kuzava
12. Roger McDowell
13. Scott McGregor
14. Alan Mills
15. Billy O'Dell
16. Robin Roberts
17. Jeff Schneider
18. Jerry Walker

Twelve Oriole Starting Pitchers Named Mike

	Starts	*Complete Games*
1. Flanagan	328	98
2. Cuellar	283	133
3. Mussina	223	35
4. Boddicker	180	48
5. Torrez	36	16
6. McCormick	23	2
7. Fornieles	15	2
8. Morgan	10	2
9. Oquist	9	0
10. Griffin	6	1
11. Johnson	5	0
12. Adamson	4	0

5 • ALL-STARS

19 Oriole All-Star Starters

1. George Kell (3B)	1956 & 1957 (2 starts)
2. Gus Triandos (C)	1958 & 1959 (Game 1) (2)
3. Jerry Walker (P)	1959 (Game 2) (1)
4. Ron Hansen (SS)	1960 (Games 1 & 2) (2)
5. Brooks Robinson (3B)	1961 (Games 1 & 2),
	1962 (Games 1 & 2),
	1964-1968, 1971-1974 (14)
6. Jim Gentile (1B)	1962 (Games 1 & 2) (2)
7. Milt Pappas (P)	1965 (1)
8. Frank Robinson (OF)	1966, 1969-1971 (4)
9. Boog Powell (1B)	1969 & 1970 (2)
10. Davey Johnson (2B)	1970 (1)
11. Jim Palmer (P)	1970, 1972, 1977 & 1978 (4)
12. Bobby Grich (SS & 2B)	1972 & 1976 (2)
13. Steve Stone (P)	1980 (1)
14. Ken Singleton (OF)	1981 & 1982 (2)
15. Cal Ripken, Jr. (SS & 3B)	1984-1998 (15)
16. Eddie Murray (1B)	1985 & 1986 (2)
17. Terry Kennedy (C)	1987 (1)
18. Roberto Alomar (2B)	1996, 1997 & 1998 (3)
19. Brady Anderson (OF)	1996 & 1997 (2)

Five Oriole All-Star Game MVPs

1. Billy O'Dell	1958
2. Brooks Robinson	1966
3. Frank Robinson	1971
4. Cal Ripken, Jr.	1991
5. Roberto Alomar.	1998

26 Oriole All-Star Non-Starters

1. Billy Loes (P)	1957
2. Billy O'Dell (P)	1958 & 1959 (Game 2)
3. Gene Woodling (OF)	1959 (Game 2)
4. Brooks Robinson (3B)	1960, 1962 (Games 1 & 2), 1963, 1969 & 1970
5. Milt Pappas (P)	1962 (Games 1 & 2)
6. Luis Aparicio (SS)	1963
7. Norm Siebern (1B)	1964
8. Davey Johnson (2B)	1968
9. Boog Powell (1B)	1968
10. Paul Blair (OF)	1969 & 1973
11. Dave McNally (P)	1969 & 1972
12. Don Buford (OF)	1971
13. Mike Cuellar (P)	1971
14. Jim Palmer (P)	1971
15. Mark Belanger (SS)	1976
16. Ken Singleton (OF)	1977 & 1979
17. Al Bumbry (OF)	1980
18. Eddie Murray (1B)	1981, 1983 & 1984
19. Cal Ripken, Jr. (SS)	1983
20. Don Aase (P)	1986
21. Mickey Tettleton (C)	1989
22. Brady Anderson (OF)	1992
23. Mike Mussina (P)	1992 & 1994
24. Lee Smith (P)	1994
25. Randy Myers (P)	1997
26. Rafael Palmeiro (1B)	1998

21 Oriole All-Stars Who Didn't Get A Chance To Play

1. Bob Turley (P)	1954
2. Jim Wilson (P)	1955
3. Gus Triandos (C)	1957
4. Hoyt Wilhelm (P)	1959 & 1961
5. Chuck Estrada (P)	1960
6. Jim Gentile (1B)	1960 & 1961
7. Jackie Brandt (OF)	1961
8. Steve Barber (P)	1966
9. Andy Etchebarren (C)	1966 & 1967
10. Mike Cuellar (P)	1970 & 1974
11. Dave McNally (P)	1970
12. Pat Dobson (P)	1972
13. Jim Palmer (P)	1975
14. Mike Flanagan (P)	1978
15. Eddie Murray (1B)	1978
16. Don Stanhouse (P)	1979
17. Scott McGregor (P)	1981
18. Tippy Martinez (P)	1983
19. Mike Boddicker (P)	1984
20. Gregg Olson (P)	1990
21. Mike Mussina (P)	1993 & 1997

Five Oriole All-Stars Who Didn't Attend Due To Injury

1. Hoyt Wilhelm (P)	1962
2. Steve Barber (P)	1963
3. Luis Aparicio (SS)	1964
4. Davey Johnson (2B)	1969
5. Boog Powell (1B)	1971

Four Orioles Who Homered In An All-Star Game

1. Frank Robinson   1971
2. Ken Singleton   19??
3. Cal Ripken, Jr.   1991
4. Roberto Alomar.   1998

Five Orioles Who Were All-Stars Before, During And After Their Stint With The Orioles

1. Luis Aparicio	White Sox 1958-62
	Orioles 1963
	White Sox 1970
	Red Sox 1971
2. Frank Robinson	Reds 1956-67, 1959, 1961-62, 1965
	Orioles 1966, 1969-71
	Angels 1974
3. Lee Smith	Cubs 1983, 1987
	Cardinals 1991-93
	Orioles 1994
	Angels 1995
4. Hoyt Wilhelm	N.Y. Giants 1953
	Orioles 1959, 1961
	Braves 1970
5. Jim Wilson	Milwaukee Braves 1954
	Orioles 1955
	White Sox 1956

Eleven Former, Current And Future Orioles Who Were 1961 All-Stars

1. Luis Aparicio	White Sox
2. Jackie Brandt	Orioles
3. Ryne Duren	L.A. Angels
4. Mike Fornieles	Red Sox
5. Jim Gentile	Orioles
6. Mike McCormick	Giants
7. Stu Miller	Giants
8. Brooks Robinson	Orioles
9. Frank Robinson	Reds
10. Johnny Temple	Indians
11. Hoyt Wilhelm	Orioles

13 1998 Orioles Who Were Ever All-Stars (Big Deal!)

1. Roberto Alomar	Blue Jays & Orioles
2. Brady Anderson	Orioles
3. Harold Baines	White Sox & A's
4. Joe Carter	Blue Jays
5. Norm Charlton	Reds
6. Eric Davis	Reds
7. Doug Drabek	Astros
8. Ozzie Guillen	White Sox
9. Jimmy Key	Blue Jays & Yankees
10. Mike Mussina	Orioles
11. Jesse Orosco	Mets
12. Rafael Palmeiro	Cubs, Rangers & Orioles
13. Cal Ripken, Jr.	Orioles

Plus coaches Mike Flanagan and Eddie Murray

Eleven Former, Current And Future Orioles Who Were 1983 All-Stars

1.	Doug DeCinces	Angels
2.	Terry Kennedy	Padres
3.	Ron Kittle	White Sox
4.	Fred Lynn	Angels
5.	Tippy Martinez	Orioles
6.	Eddie Murray	Orioles
7.	Jesse Orosco	Mets
8.	Cal Ripken, Jr.	Orioles
9.	Lee Smith	Cubs
10.	Rick Sutcliffe	Indians
11.	Fernando Valenzuela	Dodgers

14 Former, Current And Future Orioles Who Were 1991 All-Stars

1.	Roberto Alomar	Blue Jays
2.	Harold Baines	Athletics
3.	Bobby Bonilla	Pirates
4.	Joe Carter	Blue Jays
5.	Ozzie Guillen	White Sox
6.	Pete Harnisch	Astros
7.	Jimmy Key	Blue Jays
8.	Dennis Martinez	Expos
9.	Mike Morgan	Dodgers
10.	Eddie Murray	Dodgers
11.	Rafael Palmeiro	Rangers
12.	Cal Ripken, Jr.	Orioles
13.	Chris Sabo	Reds
14.	Lee Smith	Cardinals

Four Orioles Who Have Appeared In Movies

1. Jim Palmer   *The Naked Gun*
2. Reggie Jackson *The Naked Gun*
3. Rich Dauer   *Stealing Home*
4. Jeff Tackett   *Dave*

6 • AWARDS & HALLS OF FAME

Four Oriole A.L. MVP's

1. Brooks Robinson	1964
2. Frank Robinson	1966
3. Boog Powell	1970
4. Cal Ripken, Jr.	1983 & 1991

Four Oriole A.L. Cy Young Award Winners (Baseball Writers Association Of America)

1. Mike Cuellar	1969 (tied with Denny McLain)
2. Jim Palmer	1973, 1974 & 1976
3. Mike Flanagan	1979
4. Steve Stone	1980

Seven Oriole A.L. Rookies Of The Year

1. Ron Hansen	1960 BBWAA & TSN
2. Curt Blefary	1965 BBWAA & TSN
3. Al Bumbry	1973 BBWAA & TSN
4. Eddie Murray	1977 BBWAA
5. Cal Ripken, Jr.	1982 BBWAA & TSN
6. Gregg Olson	1989 BBWAA
7. Craig Worthington	1989 TSN

Two Players Who Won Rookie Of The Year And Later Won Two MVP Awards

1. Frank Robinson	1956 Rookie of the Year (Reds)
	1961 MVP (Reds)
	1966 MVP (Orioles)
2. Cal Ripken, Jr.	1982 Rookie of the Year
	1983 MVP
	1991 MVP

Eight Cy Young Award Also-Rans

1. Mike Boddicker	4th in 1984
2. Mike Cuellar	4th in 1970
3. Dennis Martinez	5th in 1981
4. Dave McNally	2nd in 1970
	4th in 1969* and 1971
5. Mike Mussina	4th in 1992, 1994 and 1995
	5th in 1996
6. Randy Myers	4th in 1997
7. Jim Palmer	2nd in 1977 and 1982
	3rd in 1978
	5th in 1970 and 1972
8. Lee Smith	5th in 1994

* winner was an Oriole

Eleven MVP Award Also-Rans

1. Jim Gentile	3rd in 1961
2. Ron Hansen	5th in 1960
3. Dave McNally	5th in 1968
4. Eddie Murray	2nd in 1982 and 1983*
	4th in 1984
	5th in 1981 and 1985
5. Randy Myers	3rd in 1997
6. Jim Palmer	2nd in 1973
7. Boog Powell	2nd in 1969
	3rd in 1966*
8. Cal Ripken, Jr.	3rd in 1989
9. Brooks Robinson	2nd in 1966*
	3rd in 1960 and 1965
	4th in 1971
10. Frank Robinson	3rd in 1969 and 1971
11. Ken Singleton	2nd in 1979
	3rd in 1977

* *winner was an Oriole*

Nine BBWAA Rookie Of The Year Also-Rans

1. Mike Boddicker	3rd in 1983
2. Wally Bunker	2nd in 1964
3. Rocky Coppinger	4th in 1996
4. Chuck Estrada	2nd in 1960*
5. Tito Francona	2nd in 1956
6. Jim Gentile	3rd in 1960*
7. Davey Johnson	3rd in 1966
8. Craig Worthington	4th in 1989*
9. Mike Young	5th in 1984

* *winner was an Oriole*

Three Oriole A.L. Rookie Pitchers Of The Year (The Sporting News)

1. Wally Bunker   1964
2. Tom Phoebus   1967
3. Mike Boddicker   1983

Three Oriole A.L. Players Of The Year (TSN)

1. Brooks Robinson   1964
2. Frank Robinson   1966
3. Cal Ripken, Jr.   1983 & 1989

Two Oriole Major League Players Of The Year (TSN)

1. Frank Robinson   1966
2. Cal Ripken, Jr.   1983 & 1989

Four Oriole A.L. Pitchers Of The Year (TSN)

1. Chuck Estrada   1960
2. Jim Palmer   1973, 1975 & 1976
3. Mike Flanagan   1979
4. Steve Stone   1980

Four Oriole Roberto Clemente Award Winners

1. Brooks Robinson   1972
2. Ken Singleton   1982
3. Cal Ripken, Jr.   1992
4. Eric Davis   1997

Three Oriole World Series MVPs

1. Frank Robinson   1966
2. Brooks Robinson   1970
3. Rick Dempsey   1983

Two Years In Which Orioles Have Finished 1-2-3 In Major Award Balloting

1960 Rookie of the Year *(only time in history)*
      1. Ron Hansen
      2. Chuck Estrada
      3. Jim Gentile

1966 Most Valuable Player *(third time in history)*
      1. Frank Robinson
      2. Brooks Robinson
      3. Boog Powell

Four Orioles Who Won Comeback Player Of The Year

1. Boog Powell   1966
2. Jim Palmer   1975
3. Rick Sutcliffe   1992
4. Eric Davis   1998

Two Orioles Who Were Puerto Rican League MVPs

1. Elrod Hendricks   1969
2. Cal Ripken, Jr.   1980

27 Most Valuable Orioles

1. Chuck Diering	1954
2. Dave Philley	1955
3. Bob Nieman	1956
4. Billy Gardner	1957
5. Gus Triandos	1958
6. Gene Woodling	1959
7. Brooks Robinson	1960, 1962, 1964 & 1971
8. Jim Gentile	1961
9. Stu Miller	1963 & 1965
10. Frank Robinson	1966, 1967 & 1971
11. Dave McNally	1968
12. Boog Powell	1969 & 1970
13. Jim Palmer	1972 & 1973
14. Paul Blair	1974
15. Mike Cuellar	1974
16. Ken Singleton	1975, 1977 & 1979
17. Lee May	1976
18. Eddie Murray	1978, 1981, 1982, 1983, 1984, 1985 & 1988
19. Al Bumbry	1980
20. Cal Ripken, Jr.	1983, 1988, 1990 & 1991
21. Don Aase	1986
22. Larry Sheets	1987
23. Gregg Olson	1989
24. Mike Devereaux	1992
25. Chris Hoiles	1993
26. Rafael Palmeiro	1995, 1996 & 1998
27. Randy Myers	1997

Twelve Oriole Gold Glove Winners
(57 Gold Gloves)

1. Brooks Robinson (3B)	1960–1975 (16 Gold Gloves)
2. Luis Aparicio (SS)	1964 & 1966 (2)
3. Paul Blair (OF)	1967, 1969–1975 (8)
4. Mark Belanger (SS)	1969, 1971, 1973–1978 (8)
5. Davey Johnson (2B)	1969–1971 (3)
6. Bobby Grich (2B)	1973–1976 (4)
7. Jim Palmer (P)	1976–1979 (4)
8. Eddie Murray (1B)	1982–1984 (3)
9. Cal Ripken, Jr, (SS)	1991 & 1992 (2)
10. Roberto Alomar (2B)	1996 & 1998 (2)
11. Mike Mussina (P)	1996, 1997 & 1998 (3)
12. Rafael Palmeiro (1B)	1997 & 1998 (2)

Eight Oriole Team Triple Crown Winners
(led team in batting average, home runs & RBI)

1. Eddie Murray	1981, 1982, 1984, 1985, 1988
2. Frank Robinson	1966*, 1967
3. Mike Devereaux	1992
4. Jim Gentile	1961
5. Rafael Palmeiro	1994 & 1995
6. Cal Ripken, Jr.	1991
7. Ken Singleton	1979 (tied with Murray for avg.)
8. Gus Triandos	1955

* *American League Triple Crown winner*

The Orioles All Award-Winners Team

RHP	Jim Palmer	1973, 1975 & 1976 Cy Young
RHP	Steve Stone	1980 Cy Young
RHP	Mike Boddicker	1983 ALCS MVP
RHP	Doug Drabek	1990 Cy Young
LHP	Mike Cuellar	1969 Cy Young (shared with Detroit's Denny McLain)
LHP	Mike Flanagan	1979 Cy Young
LHP	Billy O'Dell	1958 All-Star Game MVP
RP	Gregg Olson	1989 Rookie of the Year
C	Rick Dempsey	1983 World Series MVP
1B	Boog Powell	1970 MVP
2B	Ron Hansen	1960 Rookie of the Year
SS	Cal Ripken, Jr.	1982 Rookie of the Year 1983 & 1991 MVP 1991 All-Star Game MVP
3B	Brooks Robinson	1964 MVP 1966 All-Star Game MVP 1970 World Series MVP
OF	Frank Robinson	1966 MVP 1966 World Series MVP 1971 All-Star Game MVP
OF	Al Bumbry	1973 Rookie of the Year
OF	Curt Blefary	1965 Rookie of the Year
DH	Eddie Murray	1977 Rookie of the Year

Nine Orioles In The Baseball Hall Of Fame

		Year Elected
1. Robin Roberts, RHP		1976
2. Frank Robinson, OF		1982
3. Brooks Robinson, 3B		1983
4. George Kell, 3B		1983
5. Luis Aparicio, SS		1984
6. Hoyt Wilhelm, RHP		1985
7. Jim Palmer, RHP		1990
8. Reggie Jackson, OF		1993
9. Earl Weaver, MGR		1996

Twelve Orioles Who Received Hall Of Fame Votes But Didn't Quite Make Cooperstown

1. Don Baylor	12 in 1994, 12 in 1995
2. Mark Belanger	16 in 1988
3. Paul Blair	8 in 1986
4. Clint Courtney	1 in 1967
5. Doug DeCinces	2 in 1993
6. Bobby Grich	11 in 1992
7. Davey Johnson	3 in 1984
8. John Lowenstein	1 in 1991
9. Lee May	2 in 1988
10. Dave McNally	29 from 1981 thru 1986
11. Milt Pappas	5 in 1979
12. Boog Powell	5 in 1983

36 Oriole Hall Of Fame Members

1. Brooks Robinson   Elected 1977
2. Frank Robinson   1977
3. Dave McNally   1978
4. Boog Powell   1979
5. Gus Triandos   1981
6. Luis Aparicio   1982
7. Mike Cuellar   1982
8. Mark Belanger   1983
9. Earl Weaver   1983
10. Paul Blair   1984
11. Paul Richards   1984
12. Milt Pappas   1985
13. Jim Palmer   1986
14. Ken Singleton   1986
15. Al Bumbry   1987
16. Steve Barber   1988
17. Jim Gentile   1989
18. Stu Miller   1989
19. Dick Hall   1989
20. Hank Bauer   1990
21. Scott McGregor   1990
22. Hal Brown   1991
23. Gene Woodling   1992
24. Don Buford   1993
25. Mike Flanagan   1994
26. George Bamberger   1995
27. Chuck Thompson   1995
28. Jerold Hoffberger   1996
29. Billy Hunter   1996
30. Cal Ripken, Sr.   1996

31. Harry Dalton   1997
32. Rick Dempsey   1997
33. Davey Johnson   1997
34. Bobby Grich   1998
35. Lee May   1998
36. Lee McPhail   1998

Ten Orioles In Latin American Halls Of Fame

1. Luis Aparicio   The Venezuela Sports Hall Of Fame
2. Bobby Avila   The Hall Of Fame Of Mexican
                        Professional Baseball
3. Chico Carrasquel   The Venezuela Sports Hall Of Fame
4. Sandy Consuegra   The Cuban Baseball Hall Of Fame
5. Mike Cuellar   The Cuban Baseball Hall Of Fame
6. Mike Fornieles   The Cuban Baseball Hall Of Fame
7. Willie Miranda   The Cuban Baseball Hall Of Fame
8. Jose Morales   The Puerto Rican Baseball
                        Hall Of Fame
9. Aurelio Rodriguez   The Hall Of Fame Of Mexican
                        Professional Baseball
10. Ozzie Virgil, Sr.   The Dominican Republic Sports
                        Hall Of Fame

7 • LEAGUE LEADERS

Four Orioles Who Led The League In Runs Batted In

1. Lee May	109 in 1976
2. Eddie Murray	78 in 1981 and 107 in 1984
3. Brooks Robinson	118 in 1964
4. Frank Robinson	141 in 1966

Three Orioles Who Led The League In Runs Scored

1. Don Buford	99 in 1971
2. Cal Ripken, Jr.	121 in 1983
3. Frank Robinson	122 in 1966

Three Orioles Who Led The League In Slugging Percentage

1. Reggie Jackson	.502 in 1976
2. Boog Powell	.606 in 1964
3. Frank Robinson	.637 in 1966

Four Oriole Catchers Who Led The League In Fielding Percentage

1. Rick Dempsey	1981 and 1983
2. Elrod Hendricks	1969 and 1975
3. Chris Hoiles	1991 and 1995

Two Oriole First Basemen Who Led The League In Fielding Percentage

1. Jim Gentile	1963
2. Eddie Murray	1981 and 1982

Six Oriole Second Basemen Who Led The League In Fielding Percentage

1. Jerry Adair   1963 and 1964
2. Rich Dauer   1981
3. Billy Gardner   1957
4. Bobby Grich   1973
5. Davey Johnson   1972
6. Bill Ripken   1992

Three Oriole Shortstops Who Led The League In Fielding Percentage

1. Luis Aparicio   1963, 1964, 1965 and 1966
2. Mark Belanger   1974, 1977 and 1978
3. Cal Ripken, Jr.   1990, 1991, 1994 and 1995

13 Years In Which An Oriole Third Baseman Led The League In Fielding Percentage

1. 1956   George Kell
2. 1960   Brooks Robinson
3. 1961   Brooks Robinson
4. 1962   Brooks Robinson
5. 1963   Brooks Robinson
6. 1964   Brooks Robinson
7. 1966   Brooks Robinson
8. 1967   Brooks Robinson
9. 1968   Brooks Robinson
10. 1969   Brooks Robinson
11. 1972   Brooks Robinson
12. 1975   Brooks Robinson
13. 1998   Cal Ripken, Jr.

The All-Led-The-League-In-Fielding-Percentage-In-1963 Infield

First Base   Jim Gentile (.995)
Second Base   Jerry Adair (.994)
Shortstop   Luis Aparicio (.983)
Third Base   Brooks Robinson (.976)

Three Oriole Outfielders Who Led The League In Fielding Percentage

1. John Lowenstein   1982
2. Gary Roenicke   1980
3. Ken Singleton   1981

Six League Batting Categories Led By Frank Robinson In 1966

1. Runs   122
2. Home Runs   49
3. Run Batted In   141
4. Batting Average   .316
5. On Base Percentage   .415
6. Slugging Percentage   .637

Three Orioles Who Lead The Majors In Games Played At Their Positions

1. Brooks Robinson   2,870 games at third base
2. Luis Aparicio   2,581 games at shortstop
                      (Cal Ripken, Jr. is third at shortstop
                      with 2,302 games)
3. Eddie Murray   2,413 games at first base

Two Dubious Categories With Orioles At Number One And Number Two In 1998

1. Opponents Stolen Base Percentage (Major League)
        Chris Hoiles   .786
        Lenny Webster   .766
2. Worst Batting Average Versus Lefties (A.L.)
        Brady Anderson   .179
        Mike Bordick   .184

8 • ACHIEVEMENTS

Nine All-Time Third Base Records Held By Brooks Robinson

1. Most games at third base	2,870
2. Highest fielding average	.971
3. Most seasons leading the league in fielding average	12
4. Most chances accepted	8,902
5. Most putouts	2,697
6. Most assists	6,205
7. Most seasons leading the league in assists	8
8. Most double plays	618
9. Most Gold Gloves	16

Two All-Time Orioles Batting Totals With Brooks In First Place And Cal In Second Place

	Brooks	*Cal*
1. Games	2,986	2,704
2. At Bats	10,654	10,433

Five All-Time Orioles Batting Totals With Cal In First Place And Brooks In Second Place

	Cal	*Brooks*
1. Runs	1,510	1,232
2. Hits	2,878	2,848
2. Doubles	544	482
3. Total Bases	4,662	4,270
4. RBI	1,514	1,357
5. Extra-Base Hits	972	818

Seven All-Time Orioles Batting Records With Eddie Murray In Third Place (Behind Brooks And Cal)

1. At Bats	7,075
2. Runs	1,084
3. Hits	2,080
4. Doubles	363
5. Total Bases	3,522
6. RBI	1,224
7. Extra-Base Hits	731

Four Orioles Who Hit Four Extra Base Hits In One Game

1. Charlie Lau	July 13, 1962 (4 2B)
2. Don Baylor	April 6, 1973 (3 2B, 1 HR)
3. Dave Duncan	June 30, 1975 (4 2B)
4. Cal Ripken, Jr.	September 3, 1983 (2 2B, 2 HR)

Two Orioles Who Hit Two Doubles In One Inning

1. Mark Belanger	August 18, 1969
2. Phil Bradley	August 30, 1989

Two Orioles Who Struck Out Twice In One Inning

1. Boog Powell	July 19, 1966
2. Randy Milligan	April 21, 1992

Three Orioles Who Struck Out
At Least Five Times In One Game

1. Sam Horn   Six times on July 17, 1991
2. Don Buford   Five times on August 26, 1971
3. Phil Bradley   Five times on September 7, 1989

Four Orioles Struck Out By Texas Ranger
Bobby Witt In The Second Inning
On August 2, 1987

1. Ray Knight
2. Terry Kennedy
3. Mike Young
4. Ken Gerhart

Two Oriole Pitchers Who Walked Twelve
Batters In A Nine-Inning Game

1. Bob Turley   July 25, 1954
2. Jack Fisher   August 30, 1961

Four No-Hit Bids Broken Up By Al Bumbry

1. June 10, 1975   Jim Perry of the A's
2. May 24, 1976   Dennis Eckersley and
                        Stan Thomas of the Indians
3. August 16, 1983   John Butcher of the Rangers
4. September 15, 1984   Bob Gibson of the Brewers

Six Oriole Catchers Who Had To Fill In At First Base

1. Rick Dempsey   2 games at first base
2. Elrod Hendricks 8 games
3. Chris Hoiles   19 games
4. Bob Melvin   1 game
5. John Orsino   13 games
6. Mickey Tettleton 5 games

Five Orioles Who Appeared In Just One Game in the Majors

1. Roger Marquis (OF, 1955)   1 AB, 0 H, .000 AVG
2. Gordie Sundin (RHP, 1956)   0 IP, 0 H, 2 BB, ∞ ERA
3. George Werley (RHP, 1956)   1 IP, 1 H, 2 BB, 9.00 ERA
4. Tom Patton (C, 1957)   2 AB, 0 H, 2 SO, .000 AVG
5. Jeff Rineer (LHP, 1979)   1 IP, 0 H, 0 BB, 0.00 ERA

Thirteen Players Who Appeared In Only One Game As An Oriole

1. Vern Bickford (RHP, 1954)   4 IP, 5 H, 1 BB, 9.00 ERA
2. Ryne Duren (RHP, 1954)   2 IP, 3 H, 1 BB, 9.00 ERA
3. Chuck Essegian (OF, 1961)   1 AB, 0 H, .000 AVG
4. Ed Farmer (RHP, 1977)   0 IP, 1 H, 1 BB, ∞ ERA
5. Gene Green (OF-C, 1960)   4 AB, 1 H, .250 AVG
6. Roger Marquis (OF, 1955)   1 AB, 0 H, .000 AVG
7. Randy Miller (RHP, 1977)   ⅔ IP, 4 H, 0 BB, 40.50 ERA
8. Tom Patton (C, 1957)   2 AB, 0 H, 2 SO, .000 AVG
9. Del Rice (C, 1960)   1 AB, 0 H, .000 AVG
10. Jeff Rineer (LHP, 1979)   1 IP, 0 H, 0 BB, 0.00 ERA
11. Gordie Sundin (RHP, 1956)   0 IP, 0 H, 2 BB, ∞ ERA
12. Ozzie Virgil (3B, 1962)   0 AB, 0 H, 1 BB, no AVG
13. George Werley (RHP, 1956)   1 IP, 1 H, 2 BB, 9.00 ERA

Six Orioles Who Stole Home Against A Once Or Future Oriole Catcher

1. Tito Francona – 8/6/56 vs. Chicago's Les Moss
   (who was with the Orioles 1954-55)
2. Willie Miranda – 9/23/56 vs. Washington's
   Clint Courtney (Orioles 1954, 1960-61)
3. Al Pilarcik – 7/11/57 vs. Cleveland's Dick Brown
   (Orioles 1963-65)
4. Brooks Robinson – 8/15/59 vs. Washington's
   Clint Courtney (Orioles 1954, 1960-61)
5. Jackie Brandt – 5/24/62 vs. Detroit's Dick Brown
   (Orioles 1963-65)
6. Davey Johnson – 8/27/68 vs. Oakland's Dave Duncan
   (Orioles 1975-76)

Seven Orioles Who Stole Home More Than Once

1. Brooks Robinson   4
2. Mark Belanger   2
3. Bob Grich   2
4. Davey Johnson   2
5. Willie Miranda   2
6. Al Pilarcik   2
7. Gary Roenicke   2

Ten Major League Team Records Held (*Or Tied) By The Orioles

1. Only team to qualify for the post-season with a team ERA over 5.00 (5.14 in 1996)
2. Most consecutive games won from one opponent (23 wins over the Kansas City Royals from 5/10/69 to 8/12/70)
3. Only team to have eight runs scored against them at the beginning of a game three times (Indians 7/6/54, Yankees 4/24/60 and 9/25/90)
4. Fewest singles in a season (811 in 162 games in 1968)
5. Most home runs on the road in a season (136 in 81 games in 1996)
6. Most players with 20 or more home runs in a season (7 in 1996 – Anderson, 50; Palmeiro, 39; Bonilla , 28; Ripken, 26; Hoiles, 25; Alomar, 22; Surhoff, 21)
7. Most home runs in one month (58 in May 1987)
8. Most consecutive years with at least one pitcher winning 20 or more games (13 from 1968 through 1980)
9. Most consecutive years winning 100 or more games (3 in 1969, 1970 and 1971)
10. Most consecutive games lost at the start of a season (21 in 1988)

Eleven American League Team Records Held (*Or Tied) By The Orioles

1. Most consecutive singles in an inning (eight versus Texas in the first inning on 5/18/90)*
2. Most home runs by pinch-hitters in a season (11 in 1982)
3. Most grand slams in a season (11 in 1996)*
4. Most consecutive shutout games won in a season (5 in 1974 and 1975)
5. Most consecutive innings shut out opponent in a season (54 innings 9/1/74 through 9/7/74)
6. Most consecutive years with a no-hit game by pitchers (3, 1967, Barber/Miller; 1968, Phoebus; 1969, Palmer)*
7. Fewest hit batsmen by pitchers in a 162-game season (10 in 1983)
8. Most games won over two consecutive 162-game seasons (217 in 1969 and 1970)
9. Most games won over three consecutive 162-game seasons (318 in 1969, 1970 and 1971)
10. Most consecutive games lost in a season (21 in 1988)
11. Lowest percentage of games won in one month (.043 in April 1988, won 1, lost 22)

Four Miscellaneous Oriole Major League Records

1. Most home runs leading off a game in a season – 12 by Brady Anderson in 1996
2. Most wins in a season by a teenager – 19 by Wally Bunker in 1964
3. Most seasons with the same team – 23 by Brooks Robinson (tied with Boston's Carl Yastrzemski)
4. Most consecutive games without being caught stealing – 1,206 by Gus Triandos (Triandos was successful in his one career steal attempt, 1958)

Seven *Other* Major League Records Held By Cal Ripken, Jr.

1. Most consecutive games at shortstop – 2,216 (7/1/82 to 7/15/96)
2. Most consecutive errorless games at shortstop – 95 (4/14/90 to 7/27/90)
3. Most consecutive errorless chances at shortstop – 431
4. Most consecutive innings played – 5,342
5. Most years league leader in double plays at shortstop – 7
6. Only player to play every inning of every game of the regular season, League Championship Series and World Series – 1983
7. Fewest triples in a season with 600 or more at-bats – 0 in 1989

Two Orioles Who Hit For The Cycle

1. Brooks Robinson   July 15, 1960
2. Cal Ripken, Jr.   May 6, 1984

Two Future Orioles Who Hit For The Cycle In 1950 With The Detroit Tigers

1. George Kell   June 2
2. Hoot Evers   September 7

Two Future Orioles Outfielders Who Hit For The Cycle With The Cincinnati Reds (Exactly 30 Years And One Month Apart)

1. Frank Robinson   May 2, 1959
2. Eric Davis   June 2, 1989

Two Future Orioles Outfielders Who Hit For The Cycle With The Boston Red Sox

1. Fred Lynn   May 13, 1980
2. Dwight Evans   June 28, 1984

Four 1998 Orioles (Players Or Coaches) Who Were In The Top Five In Career RBI For Players Active Through The 1996 Season

1. Eddie Murray   1st with 1889 RBI
2. Cal Ripken   3rd with 1369 RBI
3. Harold Baines   4th with 1356 RBI
4. Joe Carter   5th with 1280 RBI

13 Major League Batting Records Held (*Or Shared) By An Oriole

1. Most Strikeouts In An Extra-Inning Game – 5*, Sam Horn, 7/17/91
2. Most Times Reaching Base On An Error In A Game – 3*, Phil Bradley, 8/4/89
3. Most Consecutive Games, One Or More Season – 2,632, Cal Ripken, Jr., 5/30/1982 thru 9/19/98
4. Most Consecutive Games At One Position – 2,216, Cal Ripken, Jr. (SS), 7/1/82 thru 7/14/96
5. Most Consecutive Innings, One Or More Season – 8,234, Cal Ripken, Jr., 6/5/82 thru 9/14/87
6. Most Home Runs By A Leadoff Hitter In A Season – 34, Brady Anderson, 1996
7. Most Home Runs Leading Off A Game In A Season – 12, Brady Anderson, 1996
8. Most Consecutive Games Leading Off With A Home Run – 4, Brady Anderson, 4/18/96 thru 4/21/96
9. Most Home Runs In The Month Of April – 11*, Brady Anderson, 1996
10. Most Grand Slams In A Game – 2*, Jim Gentile, 5/9/61 and Frank Robinson, 6/26/70
11. Most Extra Inning Home Runs In A Game – 2*, Mike Young, 5/28/87
12. Most Times Hitting A Home Run Lefthanded And Righthanded In The Same Game, In A Season – 2*, Eddie Murray, 4/24/82 & 8/26/82 and 5/8/87 & 5/9/87
13. Most Consecutive Games Hitting A Home Run Left Handed And Righthanded – 2, Eddie Murray, 5/8/87 & 5/9/87

Seven ALCS Batting Records Held (*Or Tied) By John Lowenstein

1. Most home runs by a pinch hitter in a game – 1*
2. Hitting a home run in first ALCS at bat*
3. Most total bases by a pinch hitter, career – 4*
4. Most total bases by a pinch hitter, series – 4*
5. Most RBI by a pinch hitter, career – 3
6. Most RBI by a pinch hitter, series– 3
7. Most RBI by a pinch hitter, game – 3

Three ALCS Batting Records Held (*Or Tied) By Pitcher Mike Cuellar

1. Most grand slams in a game – 1*
2. Most home runs by a pitcher in a game – 1
3. Most RBI in an inning – 4

Four ALCS Batting Records Tied By Rafael Palmeiro

1. Most times reaching base safely in a game – 5
2. Most consecutive games hitting a home run – 2
3. Hitting a home run in first ALCS at bat
4. Most strike outs in a six game series – 6

Four ALCS Batting Records Held By Brooks Robinson

1. Highest batting average in a 3-game series (10 or more at bats) – .583 in 1970
2. Most singles in a 3-game series – 6 in 1969
3. Most singles in a game – 4 on 10/4/69
4. Most hits in a 3-game series – 7 in 1969 and 1970

Ten ALCS Shortstop Fielding Records Held (*Or Tied) By Orioles

1. Most games played career – 21	Mark Belanger
2. Most putouts, career – 31	Mark Belanger
3. Most putouts in one game – 6*	Mark Belanger
4. Most putouts in an inning – 3*	Mark Belanger
5. Most assists, career – 69	Mark Belanger
6. Most assists in a 3-game series – 14	Mark Belanger
7. Most chances accepted, career – 100	Mark Belanger
8. Most consecutive errorless games, career – 17	Mark Belanger
9. Most chances accepted in a 4-game series – 22	Kiko Garcia
10. Most chances accepted in a game – 11*	Kiko Garcia

Eight ALCS Pitchers Fielding Records Held (*Or Tied) By Orioles

1. Most putouts, career – 4*	Jim Palmer
2. Most assists, career – 12	Mike Cuellar
3. Most assists in a 4-game series – 5 in 1974	Mike Cuellar
4. Most assists in a 6-game series – 5 in 1997	Scott Erickson
5. Most chances accepted, career – 13	Mike Cuellar
6. Most chances accepted in a 4-game series – 5* in 1974	Mike Cuellar
7. Most chances accepted in a 6-game series – 5 in 1997	Scott Erickson
8. Most double plays, career – 2	Mike Flanagan

Two ALCS Catching Records Shared
By Rick Dempsey And Chris Hoiles

1. Most putouts in a game – 15
2. Most chances accepted in a game – 16

Three ALCS Second Base Fielding Records
Set By Roberto Alomar In 1996

1. Most assists in a 5-game series – 25
2. Most chances accepted in a 5-game series – 40
3. Most double plays in a series – 7

Nine ALCS Third Base Fielding Records
Held (*Or Tied) By Orioles

1. Most putouts in a 3-game series – 6 in 1969	Brooks Robinson
2. Most assists, career – 49	Brooks Robinson
3. Most assists in a 4-game series – 13	Brooks Robinson in 1969 Todd Cruz in 1983
4. Most assists in a 9-inning game – 6	Todd Cruz on 10/5/83
5. Most chances accepted in a 3-game series – 16 in 1969	Brooks Robinson
6. Most chances accepted in a 4-game series – 19 in 1983	Todd Cruz
7. Most chances accepted in a game – 9	Todd Cruz on 10/5/83
8. Most double plays in a series – 3 in 1997	Cal Ripken, Jr.
9. Most double plays started in a series – 3 in 1997	Cal Ripken, Jr.

Eleven ALCS First Base Fielding Records Held (*Or Tied) By Orioles

1. Most putouts in a 3-game series –
   34 in 1969   Boog Powell
2. Most putouts in a 4-game series –
   44 in 1979   Eddie Murray
3. Most putouts in a 36-game series –
   55 in 1997   Rafael Palmeiro
4. Most assists in a 4-game series –
   3* in 1979 and 1983   Eddie Murray
5. Most chances accepted in a
   3-game series – 34 in 1969   Boog Powell
6. Most chances accepted in a
   4-game series – 47 in 1979   Eddie Murray
7. Most chances accepted in a
   6-game series – 57* in 1997   Rafael Palmeiro
8. Most consecutive errorless games,
   career – 12   Boog Powell
9. Most chances without an error in
   a series – 57* in 6 games in 1997   Rafael Palmeiro
10. Most double plays in a game –
    3* on 10/6/79   Eddie Murray
11. Most errors in career – 3*   Eddie Murray

Six ALCS Second Base Fielding Records Held (*Or Tied) By Bobby Grich

1. Most putouts in a 4-game series – 13 in 1974
2. Most putouts in a 5-game series – 16 in 1973
3. Most putouts in a 9-inning game – 7 on 10/6/74
4. Most putouts in an inning – 3* on 10/11/73
5. Most chances accepted in a 4-game series – 25 in 1974
6. Most chances accepted in a 9-inning game – 12 in 1974

Four Orioles Who Hit A Home Run In Their First World Series At Bat

1. Brooks Robinson in 1966
2. Don Buford in 1969
3. Doug DeCinces in 1979
4. Jim Dwyer in 1983

One World Series Batting Record Held By Jim Palmer

1. Most walks with the bases loaded in a game – 2

The Guys-Who-At-One-Time-Played-Third-Base-After-Brooks-Retired Team (and Where They Normally Played)

C	Jeff Tackett (1992)
1B	Eddie Murray (1978, 1988)
2B	Bill Ripken (1988)
SS	Cal Ripken, Jr. (1981-82, 1997)
3B	Doug DeCinces (1977-81)
OF	John Lowenstein (1979)
OF	Gary Roenicke (1983)
OF	Juan Beniquez (1986)
DH	Larry Sheets (1986)

Three Orioles Who Played In At Least Ten Games At All Four Infield Positions

1. Bobby Grich
2. Bob Johnson
3. Chico Salmon

Four Orioles Who Played All Four Infield Positions And Played In One Game In The Outfield

1. Doug DeCinces
2. Rene Gonzales
3. Bob Johnson
4. Chico Salmon

The Spent-Their-Entire-Major-League-Career-In-An-Orioles-Uniform Team

(not including active players)

MGR	Earl Weaver
RHP	Jim Palmer
LHP	Scott McGregor
RP	Mark Williamson
C	Frank "Noodles" Zupo
1B	Jim Traber
2B	Rich Dauer
SS	Bob Bonner
3B	Brooks Robinson
OF	Bob Nelson
OF	Jim Pyburn
OF	Ken Gerhart
DH	Pete Stanicek

13 Orioles Who Played One Year In Japan

1. Jerry Adair
2. Phil Bradley
3. Doug DeCinces
4. Jim Gentile
5. Larry Harlow
6. Mike Hartley
7. Pete Incaviglia
8. Lyle Mouton
9. Tony Muser
10. Bob Nieman
11. Bob Reynolds
12. Larry Sheets
13. Mike Young

Twelve Orioles Who Played More Than One Year In Japan

1.	Willie Kirkland	6 years
2.	Mike Reinbach	5 years
3.	Don Buford	4 years
4.	Lou Jackson	3 years
5.	Jim Marshall	3 years
6.	Buddy Peterson	3 years
7.	Pete Burnside	2 years
8.	Davey Johnson	2 years
9.	Mickey McGuire	2 years
10.	Tom O'Malley	2 years
11.	Wade Rowdon	2 years
12.	Jim Traber	2 years

Two Orioles Who Played For A Major League-Record Ten Different Teams

1. Tommy Davis — Dodgers, Mets, White Sox, Pilots, Astros, Cubs, A's, Orioles, Angels, Royals
2. Mike Morgan — A's, Yankees, Blue Jays, Mariners, Orioles, Dodgers, Cubs, Cardinal, Reds, Twins

Note: The record is also shared by Ken Brett and Bob Miller.

9 • FIRSTS & LASTS

The First Five Players To Make Their Major League Debut With The Orioles

1. Chico Garcia   April 24, 1954
2. Jay Heard   April 24, 1954
3. Billy O'Dell   June 20, 1954
4. Joe Durham   September 10, 1954
5. Ryne Duren   September 25, 1954

Orioles Who Made Their Major League Debut On The Same Day

1. Chico Garcia and Jay Heard   April 24, 1954
2. Bob Alexander, Don Ferrarese,
   Don Leppert and Hal Smith   April 11, 1955
3. Ron Hansen and Jim Marshall   April 15, 1958
4. Steve Barber and Chuck Estrada   April 21, 1960
5. Andy Etchebarren and
   Dave McNally   September 26, 1962
6. Tom Fisher and Paul Gilliford   September 20, 1967
7. Fred Beene and Bobby Floyd   September 18, 1968
8. Rich Dauer and Kiko Garcia   September 11, 1976
9. Ken Gerhart and Carl Nichols   September 14, 1986
10. Juan Bell and Ben McDonald   September 6, 1989
11. Brent Bowers and
    Nerio Rodriguez   August 16, 1996

Ten Players With The Most
Opening Day Starts For The Orioles

1. Brooks Robinson   20
2. Cal Ripken, Jr.   17
3. Mark Belanger   13
4. Paul Blair   12
5. Eddie Murray   12
6. Boog Powell   12
7. Rick Dempsey   10
8. Rich Dauer   9
9. Ken Singleton   9
10. Al Bumbry   8

The All Opening-Day Team

(by position, players who have started the most Opening Day games for the Orioles)

P	Jim Palmer	7
C	Rick Dempsey	10
1B	Eddie Murray	10
2B	Rich Dauer	8
SS	Cal Ripken, Jr.	15
3B	Brooks Robinson	20
LF	Gary Roenicke	6
CF	Paul Blair	12
RF	Ken Singleton	6
DH	Ken Singleton	3
	Sam Horn	3

Eleven Different Players Who Started In Right Field for the Orioles on Opening Day 1954-1964

1. Vic Wertz   1954
2. Gene Woodling   1955
3. Dave Philley   1956
4. Carl Powis   1957
5. Al Pilarcik   1958
6. Bobby Avila   1959
7. Johnny Powers   1960
8. Russ Snyder   1961
9. Earl Robinson   1962
10. Al Smith   1963
11. Sam Bowens   1964

Bowens started again in 1965 bringing this streak to an end.

Eight Opening Day Starters Better Known At Other Positions

1. Catcher Gus Triandos   1B in 1956
2. Second Baseman Jerry Adair   SS in 1962
3. Second Baseman Davey Johnson SS in 1968
4. Outfielder Don Buford   2B in 1968
5. Outfielder Don Baylor   1B in 1974
6. First Baseman Eddie Murray   3B in 1978
7. Third Baseman Doug DeCinces   2B in 1978
8. First Baseman Randy Milligan LF in 1991

Two Oriole Players Who Started At The Most Different Positions On Opening Day

1. Eddie Murray   DH in 1977
                    3B in 1978
                    1B from 1979-88
2. John Shelby   CF in 1983 & 1984
                    LF in 1986
                    RF in 1987

Some Oriole Firsts

1. First World Series game on artificial turf – O's versus Reds on October 10, 1970.
2. First night World Series game – O's versus Pirates on October 13, 1971.
3. Dave McNally and Andy Messersmith become the first free agents.

Four Orioles Who Were The First From Their Country To Play In The Major Leagues

1. Ozzie Virgil (w/ N.Y. Giants) in 1956 Dominican Rep.
2. Dennis Martinez in 1976   Nicaragua
3. Chito Martinez in 1991   Belize
4. Eugene Kingsdale in 1996   Aruba

Orioles pitcher Tony Chevez was the second player from Nicaragua and former Orioles farmhand Calvin Maduro was the second player from Aruba (with the Phillies). The third and fourth from Aruba were O's pitchers Sidney Ponson and his cousin Radhames Dykhoff.

14 Well-Known Opposing Players Who Ended Their Careers With The Orioles

1. Nelson Briles
2. Rick Burleson
3. Walt Dropo
4. Dwight Evans
5. Hoot Evers
6. Harvey Haddix
7. Tommy Harper
8. George Kell
9. Jimmy Key
10. Eddie Lopat
11. Hank Majeski
12. Keith Moreland
13. Jim Northrup
14. Bobby Thomson

10 • BIRTH, LIFE & DEATH

The Most Common Oriole Birthdays

1. September 2	6 players
2. January 18	5 players
3. February 3	5 players
4. April 4	5 players
5. April 14	5 players
6. July 26	5 players
7. August 23	5 players
8. November 3	5 players
9. December 26	5 players

The Most Common Months For Oriole Birthdays

1. September	63
2. January	58
3. December	58
4. August	57
5. October	55

The All-Born-In-California Team

RHP	Scott Erickson
LHP	Scott McGregor
RP	Jesse Orosco
C	Andy Etchebarren
1B	Jim Gentile
2B	Rich Dauer
SS	Kiko Garcia
3B	Doug DeCinces
OF	Gary Roenicke
OF	Dan Ford
OF	Eric Davis
DH	Eddie Murray

Eleven Pairs Of Orioles Born on the Same Date

1. Art Ceccarelli and Gordon Jones	4/2/30
2. Rip Coleman and Joe Durham	7/31/31
3. Dave Nicholson and Frank "Noodles" Zupo	8/29/39
4. Tom Fisher and Eddie Watt	4/4/42
5. Bruce Howard and Lee May	3/23/43
6. Mike Hart and Alan Wiggins	2/17/58
7. Storm Davis and Jim Traber	12/26/61
8. Roger McDowell and Andy Van Slyke	12/21/60
9. Pat Clements and Paul Kilgus	2/2/62
10. Matt Nokes and Mike Smith	10/31/63
11. Mark Leonard and Tommy Shields	8/14/64

Two Orioles Born In The Same Hospital As The Author Of This Book

1. Cal Ripken, Jr.
2. Bill Ripken

17 Orioles Who Made Their Major League Debut With A Team From The City Where They Were Born

1. Damon Buford	Baltimore Orioles
2. Chuck Diering	St. Louis Cardinals
3. Ted Gray	Detroit Tigers
4. Kevin Hickey	Chicago White Sox
5. Art Houtteman	Detroit Tigers
6. Fred Holdsworth	Detroit Tigers
7. Stan Jefferson	New York Mets
8. Bob Kennedy	Chicago White Sox
9. Jim Lehew	Baltimore Orioles
10. John Miller	Baltimore Orioles
11. Tim Nordbrook	Baltimore Orioles
12. John E. O'Donoghue	Kansas City Athletics
13. Tom Phoebus	Baltimore Orioles
14. Rick Schu	Philadelphia Phillies
15. Barry Shetrone	Baltimore Orioles
16. Ken Singleton	New York Mets
17. Lou Sleater	St. Louis Browns

Eleven Cities Where The Most Orioles Were Born

1. Los Angeles	13 Orioles
2. St. Louis	12
3. Detroit	10
4. New York	9
5. Baltimore	8
6. Brooklyn	8
7. Chicago	8
8. San Diego	7
9. San Francisco	7
10. Dallas	6
11. Philadelphia	6

Twelve States Where the Most Orioles Were Born

1. California	94 Orioles
2. New York	37
3. Texas	33
4. Pennsylvania	31
5. Illinois	29
6. Michigan	28
7. Ohio	24
8. Louisiana	20
9. Maryland	20
10. Missouri	20
11. North Carolina	17
12. New Jersey	16

Six States Where One Oriole Was Born

1. Alaska	Curt Schilling
2. Nevada	Shawn Boskie
3. New Hampshire	Mike Flanagan
4. North Dakota	Mark Lee
5. Rhode Island	Art Quirk
6. Wyoming	Mike Devereaux

Four States Where No Orioles Were Born

1. Idaho
2. Maine
3. South Dakota
4. Utah

The Twelve Countries Where
The Most Orioles Were Born

1. United States	565 Orioles
2. Dominican Republic	16
3. Puerto Rico	11
4. Cuba	8
5. Mexico	7
6. Venezuela	5
7. Canada	4
8. Aruba	3
9. Virgin Islands	3
10. Germany	2
11. Nicaragua	2
12. Panama	2

Five Countries Where Only One Oriole Was Born

1. Belize
2. Colombia
3. Poland
4. Scotland
5. Spain

20 Non-Natives Who Settled In The Baltimore Area After Playing For The Orioles

1. Mark Belanger	Timonium
2. Paul Blair	Baltimore
3. Al Bumbry	Lutherville
4. Terry Crowley	Cockeysville
5. Ken Dixon	Baltimore
6. Joe Durham	Randallstown
7. Mike Flanagan	Timonium
8. Ross Grimsley	Towson
9. Ron Hansen	Baldwin
10. Elrod Hendricks	Randallstown
11. Billy Hunter	Lutherville
12. Pat Kelly	Timonium
13. Tippy Martinez	Towson
14. Scott McGregor	Towson
15. Willie Miranda	Baltimore
16. John E. O'Donoghue	Elkton
17. Jim Palmer	Brooklandville
18. Brooks Robinson	Lutherville
19. Ken Singleton	Lutherville
20. Bill Swaggerty	Hampstead

The All Born (*Or Raised) In Maryland Team

Mgr	Cal Ripken, Sr.	Aberdeen
Coa	Cal Ermer	Baltimore
Coa	Ray Miller	Takoma Park
RHP	Tom Phoebus	Baltimore
LHP	Steve Barber	Takoma Park
C	John Stefero*	Baltimore
1B	Jim Traber*	Columbia
2B	Bill Ripken	Havre de Grace
SS	Tim Nordbrook	Baltimore
3B	Cal Ripken, Jr.	Havre de Grace
OF	Brady Anderson	Silver Spring
OF	Jim Fuller	Bethesda
OF	Barry Shetrone	Baltimore
DH	Harold Baines	Easton

Reserves

P	Dave Boswell	Baltimore
OF	Damon Buford	Baltimore
OF	Leo Burke	Hagerstown
P	Jack Fisher	Frostburg
P	Dick Hall*	Towson
P	Bruce Howard	Salisbury
P	Dave Johnson	Baltimore
P	Jim Lehew	Baltimore
P	Dave Leonhard*	Baltimore
P	John Miller	Baltimore
P	Ray Moore	Meadows
P	Lou Sleater*	Baltimore
P	Garrett Stephenson	Takoma Park
2B	Bobby Young	Granite

Must Be Something In The Water

1. Three Orioles who played first base and designated hitter from the Virgin Islands
   – Elrod Hendricks, Jose Morales and Calvin Pickering
2. Two Orioles coaches from Staten Island, New York
   – George Bamberger & Terry Crowley
3. Two Orioles pitchers from Billings, Montana
   – Dave McNally & Jeff Ballard
4. Two Orioles pitchers from Havana, Cuba
   – Mike Fornieles & Marcelino Lopez
5. Two Orioles first baseman from Paris, Texas
   – Dave Philley & Eddie Robinson
6. Two Orioles shortstops from San Pedro de Macoris, Dominican Republic
   – Juan Bell & Manny Alexander (along with many more throughout the majors)

Five Orioles Born In Europe

1. Moe Drabowsky   Ozanna, Poland
2. Craig Lefferts   Munich, Germany
3. Al Pardo   Oviedo, Spain
4. Mickey Scott   Weimar, Germany
5. Bobby Thomson   Glasgow, Scotland

Two Orioles Who Sang The National Anthem At A Major League Game

1. Nelson Briles – at Shea Stadium in N.Y. before Game 4 of the 1973 World Series
2. Jim Traber – at Memorial Stadium before the O's game in which he made his major league debut (9/21/84)

Two Orioles Who Received Military Honors

1. Mgr. Hank Bauer – received two Purple Hearts and a Bronze Star as a Marine in WWII
2. Al Bumbry – received Bronze Star as a platoon leader in Vietnam

Orioles Who Missed Playing Time To Serve In The National Guard During The 1968 Riots

1. Mark Belanger (Maryland Air National Guard)
2. Dave Leonhard (Maryland Air National Guard)
3. Pete Richert (Washington, DC National Guard)

Four Orioles' High School Hi-Jinx

1. Frank Robinson – graduate of McClymonds High School in Oakland, CA, basketball teammate of former NBA star Bill Russell, and baseball teammate of Vada Pinson and Orioles Willie Tasby and Charlie Beamon
2. Lee Lacy – also a graduate of McClymonds High School
3. Scott McGregor – a teammate of Kansas City's George Brett at El Segundo High School in California and teacher at Baltimore's Gilman School
4. Eddie Murray – tri-captain of Locke High School baseball team in Los Angeles along with Cardinals shortstop Ozzie Smith and former Twins pitcher Darrell Jackson

13 Orioles' Collegiate Capers

1. Don Buford – member of All-Conference football team at USC in 1958
2. Phil Bradley – three-time All Big Eight quarterback at Missouri
3. Al Bumbry – attended Virginia State College on a basketball scholarship
4. Pete Burnside – earned bachelor's degree at Dartmouth and master's degree from Northwestern
5. Clay Dalrymple – heavyweight boxer at Chico State
6. Chuck Essegian – played in the Rose Bowl while attending Stanford
7. Dick Hall – earned 10 letters at Swarthmore College; 3 in baseball, 2 in football, 3 in basketball, 1 in soccer and 1 in track
8. Dave Leonhard – started school at Washington College in Chestertown, Maryland; received degree in history from The Johns Hopkins University
9. John Lowenstein – earned B.A. in anthropology at the University of California at Riverside
10. Al Pilarcik – earned B.S. at Valparaiso University and M.S. at Purdue University
11. Merv Rettenmund – drafted by the Dallas Cowboys out of Ball State in 1964
12. Tim Stoddard – was forward on N.C. State's National Championship basketball team in 1974
13. Jim Traber – starting quarterback at Oklahoma State in 1980

Nineteen Orioles Who Had "Spirited" Post-Baseball Careers

1. Cal Abrams – owned and operated Cal Abrams' Dugout in Garden City, New York

2. Hank Bauer – owned and operated a liquor store in the Kansas City area
3. Dave Boswell – worked for the National Brewing Co. in Baltimore
4. Leo Burke – owned and operated Leo Burke's Colonial Liquors in Hagerstown, Maryland
5. Angie Dagres – owned and operated a bar and restaurant in Massachusetts
6. Joe Durham – worked as a salesman for Churchill Distributors, a liquor distributor in Baltimore
7. Chico Fernandez – worked for the National Brewing Co. in Florida
8. Don Ferrarese – owned and operated Hugo's Liquor Store & Deli in Apple Valley, California
9. Howie Fox – owned a tavern in San Antonio, Texas (was stabbed to death in tavern in 1955)
10. Joe Ginsberg – was a Jack Daniel's sales representative
11. Gene Green – managed Mr. Frank's Cocktail Lounge in St. Louis
12. Bob Johnson – worked as a sales representative for a liquor wholesaler in Minneapolis
13. Stu Miller – owned and operated Ernie's Liquors in San Carlos, California
14. John E. O'Donoghue – owned and managed a nightclub in Newark, Delaware
15. Tom Phoebus – worked for Churchill Distributors
16. Al Smith – owned and operated a tavern
17. Russ Snyder – owned and operated the Sportsman's Tavern & Steakhouse in Nelson, Nebraska
18. Vic Wertz – owned a beer distributorship in the Detroit area
19. Frank "Noodles" Zupo – managed the Pro Club Cocktail Lounge in Millbrae, California

The Three Most Common Oriole Dates of Demise

1. January 9	Johnny Temple	1994
	Jim Fridley	1996
2. April 9	Disk Kokos	1996
	Joe Coleman	1997
3. September 2	Jim Wilson	1986
	Camilo Carreon	1987

Two Orioles Who Died In Plane Crashes

1. Tom Gastall	1956
2. Jim Hardin	1991

Nine Orioles Who Died In The Same Town In Which They Were Born

1. Dave Koslo	Menasha, WI
2. Frank Kellert	Oklahoma City, OK
3. Jim Finigan	Quincy, IL
4. Harry Byrd	Darlington, SC
5. Dick Kokos	Chicago, IL
6. Alan Wiggins	Los Angeles, CA
7. Hank Majeski	Staten Island, NY
8. Marlin Stuart	Paragould, AR
9. Gene Brabender	Madison, WI

The All-Deceased Team

MGR	Paul Richards	d. 5/4/86
SP	Jim Hardin	d. 3/9/91
RP	Harvey Haddix	d.1/8/94
C	Dick Brown	d. 4/12/70
1B	Eddie Waitkus	d. 9/15/72
2B	Bobby Young	d. 1/28/85
SS	Willie Miranda	d. 9/7/96
3B	Vern Stephens	d. 1/3/68
OF	Bob Nieman	d. 3/10/85
OF	Jim Busby	d. 7/8/96
OF	Hoot Evers	d. 1/25/91
DH	Alan Wiggins	d. 1/6/91

Six Dead Batteries (And The Years They Were with the O's)

1. Pitcher Joe Coleman & Catcher Clint Courtney	1954
2. Pitcher Ray Moore & Catcher Tom Gastall	1955-56
3. Pitcher Gordon Jones & Catcher Del Rice	1960
4. Pitcher George Brunet & Catcher Dick Brown	1963
5. Pitcher Harvey Haddix & Catcher Charlie Lau	1964-65
6. Pitcher Gene Brabender & Catcher Camilo Carreon	1966

11 • FAMILIES

Seven Oriole Families

1. Cal Ripken, Sr. and sons Cal, Jr. and Bill
2. Bob Kennedy (1954) and son Terry (1987-88)
3. Brothers Dick (1963-65) and Larry Brown (1973)
4. Don Buford (1968-72) and son Damon (1993-95)
5. John E. O'Donoghue (1968) and son John P. (1993-94)
6. Rick Dempsey (1976-86, 1992) and nephew Greg Zaun (1995-96)
7. Sidney Ponson (1998) and cousin Radhames Dykhoff (1998)

Two Orioles With Famous Ancestors

1. Dan Boone (1990) is the 7th generation nephew of frontiersman Daniel Boone.
2. Rick Dempsey (1976-86, 1992) is a distant relative of boxer Jack Dempsey.

33 Orioles With A Relative Who Played In The Major Leagues (But Not With The Orioles)

1. Bobby Adams (1956), brother Dick and son Mike
2. Roberto Alomar (1996-98), brother Sandy, Jr. and father Sandy, Sr.
3. Mike Anderson (1978) and brother Kent
4. Charlie Beamon (1956-58) and son Charlie, Jr.
5. Juan Bell (1989-91) and brother George
6. Camilo Carreon (1966) and son Mark
7. Joe Coleman (1954-55) and son Joe
8. Tito Francona (1956-57) and son Terry
9. Ross Grimsley (1974-77 and 1982) and father Ross
10. Jerry Hairston (1998) and father Jerry, Uncle Johnny and Grandfather Sam
11. Larry Haney (1966-68) and son Chris
12. Bruce Howard (1968) and son David
13. George Kell (1956-57) and brother Skeeter
14. Billy Klaus (1959-60) and brother Bobby
15. Dave May (1967-70) and son Derrick
16. Lee May (1975-80) and brother Carlos
17. Jeff McKnight (1990-91) and father Jim
18. John Mitchell (1990) and brother Charlie
19. Eddie Murray (1977-88) and brother Rich
20. Donell Nixon (1990) and brother Otis
21. Bob Oliver (1974) and son Darren
22. Dee Pillette (1954-55) and father Herman
23. Boog Powell (1961-74) and step-brother Carl Taylor
24. Harold Reynolds (1993) and brother Don
25. Gary Roenicke (1978-85) and brother Ron

26. David Segui (1990-93) and father Diego
27. Pete Stanicek (1987-88) and brother Steve
28. B.J. Surhoff (1996-98) and brother Rich
29. Marv Throneberry (1961-62) and brother Faye
30. Dizzy Trout (1957) and son Steve
31. Tom Underwood (1984) and brother Pat
32. Ozzie Virgil (1962) and son Ozzie, Jr.
33. Wally Westlake (1955) and brother Jim

Three Orioles With A Football-Playing Relative

1. Frank Baker – brother John was a linebacker with Houston and San Diego of the old AFL
2. Pat Kelly – brother Leroy was an All-Pro running back with the Cleveland Browns
3. Ken Singleton – uncle Harvey Singleton was a tackle for the Toronto Argonauts of the CFL

One Oriole With A Basketball-Playing Relative

1. B.J. Surhoff – father Dick played for the New York Knicks

12 • PHYSICAL

The Ten Tallest Orioles*

1.	Rich Bordi	6'7"
2.	Ben McDonald	6'7"
3.	Tim Stoddard	6'7"
4.	Rick Sutcliffe	6'7"
5.	Dick Hall	6'6½"
6.	Stacy Jones	6'6"
7.	John O'Donoghue	6'6"
8.	Brad Pennington	6'6"
9.	Jeff Robinson	6'6"
10.	Lee Smith	6'6"

The 17 Shortest Orioles*

1.	Albie Pearson	5'5"
2.	Jarvis Brown	5'7"
3.	Jehosie Heard	5'7"
4.	Curt Motton	5'7"
5.	Dan Boone	5'8"
6.	Don Buford	5'8"
7.	Al Bumbry	5'8"
8.	Rich Coggins	5'8"
9.	Clint Courtney	5'8"
10.	Dave Criscione	5'8"
11.	Chico Garcia	5'8"
12.	Dick Kokos	5'8"
13.	Don Leppert	5'8"
14.	Chuck Oertel	5'8"
15.	Tom Phoebus	5'8"
16.	Luis Polonia	5'8"
17.	John Stefero	5'8"

*according to *Total Baseball: The Official Encyclopedia of Major League Baseball*

The Nine Heaviest Orioles*

1. Rocky Coppinger	250 lbs.
2. Mike Epstein	250 lbs.
3. Sam Horn	250 lbs.
4. Tim Stoddard	250 lbs.
5. Boog Powell	240 lbs.
6. Jeff Robinson	240 lbs.
7. Bobby Bonilla	230 lbs.
8. Randy Milligan	230 lbs.
9. Esteban Yan	230 lbs.

The Four Lightest Orioles*

1. Albie Pearson	141 lbs.
2. Dan Boone	150 lbs.
3. Billy Cox	150 lbs.
4. Willie Miranda	150 lbs.
5. Luis De Leon	153 lbs.
6. Orlando Pena	154 lbs.
7. Jehosie Heard	155 lbs.
8. Luis Polonia	155 lbs.

*according to *Total Baseball: The Official Encyclopedia of Major League Baseball*

The Eight Oldest Orioles To Appear In A Game

1. Rick Dempsey	43 years
2. Dizzy Trout	42 years 2 months
3. Dave Philley	41 years 4 months
4. Jesse Orosco	41 years 5 months
5. Dick Hall	40 years 11 months
6. Eddie Murray	40 years 5 months
7. Mike Flanagan	40 years 9 months
8. Brooks Robinson	40 years 3 months

The Nine Youngest Orioles To Appear In A Game

1. Frank "Noodles" Zupo	17 years 10 months 2 days
2. Ron Moeller	17 years 10 months 26 days
3. George Werley	18 years 21 days
4. Milt Pappas	18 years 2 months 30 days
5. Bob Saverine	18 years 3 months 10 days
6. Brooks Robinson	18 years 3 months 30 days
7. Jerry Walker	18 years 4 months 24 days
8. Wayne Causey	18 years 5 months 11 days
9. Roger Marquis	18 years 5 months 20 days

The All Teen-Age Team

RHP	Wally Bunker	18 in 1963
LHP	Dave McNally	19 in 1962
C	Andy Etchebarren	19 in 1962
1B	Boog Powell	19 in 1961
2B	Bob Saverine	18 in 1959
SS	Wayne Causey	18 in 1955
3B	Brooks Robinson	18 in 1955
OF	Boog Powell	19 in 1961
OF	Bob Nelson	18 in 1955
OF	Roger Marquis	18 in 1955

Reserves

P	Mike Adamson	19 in 1967
P	Ed Barnowski	19 in 1965
P	Ron Moeller	17 in 1956
P	Jim Palmer	19 in 1965
P	Gordie Sundin	18 in 1956
P	Jerry Walker	18 in 1957
P	George Werley	18 in 1956
C	Frank "Noodles" Zupo	17 in 1957

Seven Things That Andy Etchebarren And Frank Zupo Have In Common

1. Born in California
2. Played for the Baltimore Orioles
3. Still in their teens when they played their first major league game
4. Were catchers
5. Had silly nicknames (Etchebarren was called "Lurch," Zupo was called "Noodles")
6. Now live in California
7. Uni-brow

The All Eyeglass-Wearing Team

Mgr	Frank Robinson
RHP	Gene Brabender
LHP	Rudy May
C	Clint Courtney
1B	Eddie Murray*
2B	Jim Finigan
SS	Lenn Sakata
3B	Chris Sabo
OF	John Lowenstein
OF	Reggie Jackson
OF	Dan Ford
DH	Ron Kittle

Reserves

P	Ryne Duren
3B	Leo Gomez
P	Dick Hyde
IF	Jeff McKnight
P	Roger Nelson
C	Joe Nolan
IF	Kelly Paris
P	Mike Parrott
SS	Buddy Peterson
P	Bill Scherrer
P	Dorn Taylor
P	Dizzy Trout

*Okay, okay—Eddie Murray never wore glasses to play while he was with the Orioles. But the majority of the talk show callers during his first Orioles stint thought he should wear glasses. Besides, he did put his specs on long enough to have his photo taken for his 1987 Topps™ baseball card. You could look it up.

Two Orioles With Mustaches Who Led A Japanese League In RBI

1. Jim Traber   92 RBI in 1991 (Pacific League)
2. Larry Sheets   100 RBI in 1992 (Central League)

The All-Moustache Team

MGR	Johnny Oates
COA	Elrod Hendricks
RHP	Dennis Martinez
LHP	Mike Flanagan
RP	Sammy Stewart
C	Rick Dempsey
1B	Rafael Palmeiro
2B	Rich Dauer
SS	Bobby Grich
3B	Doug DeCinces
OF	Al Bumbry
OF	John Lowenstein
OF	Gary Roenicke
DH	Larry Sheets

The All-Switch-Hitting Team

RHP	Scott McGregor
LHP	Robin Roberts
RP	Alan Mills
C	Mickey Tettleton
1B	Eddie Murray
2B	Roberto Alomar
SS	Willie Miranda
3B	Bobby Bonilla
OF	Don Buford
OF	John Shelby
OF	Mike Young
DH	Ken Singleton

13 • MANAGERS & COACHES

The Orioles-Who-Became-
Big-League-Managers Team

P	George Bamberger	Mets & Brewers
C	Johnny Oates	Orioles & Rangers
1B	Whitey Lockman	Cubs
2B	Davey Johnson	Mets, Reds & Orioles
SS	Billy Hunter	Rangers
3B	Ray Knight	Reds
OF	Whitey Herzog	Rangers, Angels, Royals & Cardinals
OF	Don Baylor	Rockies
OF	Lou Piniella	Yankees, Reds & Mariners
DH	Frank Robinson	Indians, Giants & Orioles

Reserves

OF	Joe Frazier	Mets
2B	Billy Gardner	Twins & Royals
IF	Grady Hatton	Astros
C	Darrell Johnson	Red Sox, Mariners & Rangers
3B	Bob Kennedy	Cubs & A's
P	Eddie Lopat	A's
1B	Jim Marshall	Cubs & A's
OF	Sam Mele	Twins
C	Les Moss	White Sox & Tigers
1B	Tony Muser	Royals
C	Del Rice	Angels
OF	Dick Williams	Red Sox, A's, Angels, Expos, Padres & Mariners

Seven Oriole Managers Of The Year

1. Paul Richards	1960 UPI
2. Hank Bauer	1964 AP
	1966 AP & TSN
3. Earl Weaver	1973 AP
	1977 AP & TSN
	1979 API, TSN & UPI
4. Joe Altobelli	1983 UPI
5. Frank Robinson	1989 BBWAA, TSN & UPI
6. Johnny Oates	1993 TSN
7. Davey Johnson	1997 BBWAA & TSN

Two Teams That Have Been Managed By More Former Orioles Than The O's Have

1. Rangers	Whitey Herzog, Billy Hunter, Darrell Johnson and Johnny Oates
2. A's	Eddie Lopat, Bob Kennedy, Dick Williams and Jim Marshall

Six Teams Never Managed By A Former Oriole Player

1. Blue Jays
2. Braves
3. Dodgers (through 1998)
4. Phillies*
5. Pirates
6. Marlins

The Phillies are managed by Terry Francona, the son of former Oriole Tito Francona.

Seven Orioles Who Played First Base And Outfield For The O's And Later Managed In The Bigs

1. Don Baylor
2. Bob Kennedy
3. Whitey Lockman
4. Jim Marshall
5. Tony Muser
6. Frank Robinson
7. Dick Williams

The All-Oriole-Coaches-Who-Were-Also-Oriole-Players Team

RHP	Pat Dobson
LHP	Mike Flanagan
C	Elrod Hendricks
1B	Eddie Murray
2B	Don Buford
SS	Billy Hunter
3B	Brooks Robinson
OF	Frank Robinson
OF	Al Bumbry
OF	Gene Woodling
DH	Terry Crowley

Twelve Orioles Coaches Who Never Played In The Majors

1. Carlos Bernhardt
2. Greg Biagini
3. Rick Down
4. Jim Frey
5. John Hart
6. Vern Hoscheit
7. Ray Miller
8. Cal Ripken, Sr.
9. Ralph Rowe
10. Al Vincent
11. Earl Weaver
12. Jimmy Williams

The Five States Where the Most Orioles Managers And Coaches Were Born

1. Texas   8
2. Michigan   6
3. Alabama   5
4. North Carolina   5
5. Maryland   4

Three Orioles Managers Or Coaches Who Died In The Same Town In Which They Were Born

1. Jimmy Dykes	Philadelphia, PA (Dykes also made his major league debut in 1918 with the Philadelphia Athletics.)
2. Tom Oliver	Montgomery, AL
3. Paul Richards	Waxahachie, TX

14 • TRADES & DRAFTS

Three Players Who Had Three Tours Of Duty With The Orioles

1. Clint Courtney   1954 Orioles
                       1955-59 White Sox & Senators
                       1960 Orioles
                       1961 K.C. A's
                       1961 Orioles
2. Elrod Hendricks   1968-72 Orioles
                       1972 Cubs
                       1973-76 Orioles
                       1976-77 Yankees
                       1978-79 Orioles
3. Dick Williams   1956-57 Orioles
                       1957 Indians
                       1958 Orioles
                       1959-60 K.C. A's
                       1961-62 Orioles

28 Players Who Had Two Tours
Of Duty With The Orioles

1. Harold Baines	1993-95 Orioles
	1996-97 White Sox
	1997-98 Orioles
2. Frank Bertaina	1964-67 Orioles
	1967-69 Senators
	1969 Orioles
3. Jim Brideweser	1954 Orioles
	1955-56 White Sox & Tigers
	1957 Orioles
4. Jim Busby	1957-58 Orioles
	1959-60 Red Sox
	1960-61 Orioles
5. Terry Crowley	1969-73 Orioles
	1974-76 Reds & Braves
	1976-82 Orioles
6. Storm Davis	1982-86 Orioles
	1987-91 Padres, A's & Royals
	1992 Orioles
7. Rick Dempsey	1976-86 Orioles
	1987-91 Indians, Dodgers & Brewers
	1992 Orioles
8. Mike Devereaux	1989-94 Orioles
	1995 White Sox & Braves
	1996 Orioles
9. Moe Drabowsky	1966-68 Orioles
	1969-70 Royals
	1970 Orioles
10. Hoot Evers	1955 Orioles
	1955-56 Indians
	1956 Orioles
11. Mike Flanagan	1975-87 Orioles
	1987-90 Blue Jays
	1991-92 Orioles

12. John Flinn	1978-79 Orioles
	1980 Brewers
	1982 Orioles
13. Lenny Green	1957-59 Orioles
	1959-64 Senators, Twins &
	L.A. Angels
	1964 Orioles
14. Ross Grimsley	1974-77 Orioles
	1978-80 Expos & Indians
	1982 Orioles
15. Dick Hall	1961-66 Orioles
	1967-68 Phillies
	1969-71 Orioles
16. Tito Landrum	1983 Orioles
	1984-87 Cardinals & Dodgers
	1988 Orioles
17. Don Larsen	1954 Orioles
	1955-65 Yankees, K.C. A's,
	White Sox, Giants & Colt .45s/Astros
	1965 Orioles
18. Richie Lewis	1992 Orioles
	1993-95 Marlins
	1996 Tigers
	1998 Orioles
19. Charlie Lau	1961-63 Orioles
	1963-64 K.C. A's
	1964-67 Orioles
20. Curt Motton	1967-71 Orioles
	1972 Brewers & Angels
	1973-74 Orioles
21. Eddie Murray	1977-88 Orioles
	1989-96 Dodgers, Mets & Indians
	1996 Orioles

22. Mark Parent	1992-93 Orioles
	1994-96 Cubs, Pirates & Tigers
	1996 Orioles
23. Dave Philley	1955-56 Orioles
	1956-60 White Sox, Tigers,
	Phillies & Giants
	1960-61 Orioles
24. Floyd Rayford	1980, 1982 Orioles
	1983 Cardinals
	1984-87 Orioles
25. Bill Ripken	1987-92 Orioles
	1993-95 Rangers & Indians
	1996 Orioles
26. Don Stanhouse	1978-79 Orioles
	1980 Dodgers
	1982 Orioles
27. Fred Valentine	1959, 1963 Orioles
	1964-68 Senators
	1968 Orioles
28. Gene Woodling	1955 Orioles
	1955-57 Indians
	1958-60 Orioles

Seven Players Traded for Elrod Hendricks

1. Tommy Davis	from Cubs to Orioles (8/18/72)
2. Francisco Estrada	to Cubs from Orioles (10/30/72)
3. Rick Dempsey	from Yankees to Orioles (6/15/76)
4. Tippy Martinez	from Yankees to Orioles (6/15/76)
5. Rudy May	from Yankees to Orioles (6/15/76)
6. Scott McGregor	from Yankees to Orioles (6/15/76)
7. Dave Pagan	from Yankees to Orioles (6/15/76)

Eight Interesting Trades

1. **The Famous 17-Player Deal** (11/8/54 to 12/3/54). The Orioles sent pitchers Mike Blyzka, Don Larsen and Bob Turley, catcher Darrell Johnson, infielders Billy Hunter and Dick Kryhoski, and outfielders Ted del Guercio and Jim Fridley to the New York Yankees in exchange for pitchers Harry Byrd, Jim McDonald and Bill Miller, catchers Hal Smith and Gus Triandos, infielders Don Leppert, Kal Segrist and Willie Miranda, and outfielder Gene Woodling.

2. **Green and Pearson Trade Places Overnight.** Outfielder Lenny Green was with the Orioles the night of 5/26/59 when they beat the Senators in the first game of a series in Baltimore. During the night he was swapped to the Senators for outfielder Albie Pearson.

3. **Clint Courtney Traded for Himself.** In January of 1961, catcher Clint Courtney was traded to the Kansas City Athletics with Al Pilarcik, Bob Boyd, Jim Archer and Wayne Causey in exchange for Whitey Herzog, Russ Snyder and a player to be named later. In April the trade was completed when Courtney, after having played in one game for the A's, was sent back to the Orioles as the player to be named later.

4. **Green Swapped Overnight Again.** In September, 1964, Angels outfielder Lenny Green was with the California club for the first game of a series with the Orioles. During the night he was dealt to Baltimore and was in uniform with the Birds for the second game of the series.

5. **The Trades for the Trade, and the Trade.** In early December, 1965, outfielder Jackie Brandt and pitcher Darold Knowles were traded to the Philadelphia Phillies for pitcher Jack Baldschun. Around the same

time, first baseman Norm Siebern was traded to the California Angels for outfielder Dick Simpson. A few days later, on December 9th, Baldschun, Simpson and pitcher Milt Pappas were sent to the Cincinnati Reds in exchange for outfielder Frank Robinson, who was then considered "an old 30."

6. **The Famous 10-Player Deal** (6/15/76). The Orioles swapped pitchers Doyle Alexander, Ken Holtzman (who hated playing in Baltimore), Grant Jackson and Jimmy Freeman and catcher Elrod Hendricks to the New York Yankees (of the Famous 17-Player Deal) for pitchers Scott McGregor, Tippy Martinez, Rudy May and Dave Pagan and catcher Rick Dempsey.

7. **The "Where Are They Now?" Trade I** (12/4/88). First baseman Eddie Murray was traded to the Los Angeles Dodgers for pitchers Brian Holton and Ken Howell and shortstop Juan Bell. Murray averaged 21 home runs and 80 RBI with the Dodgers, Mets, Indians and O's from 1989 through 1996 before retiring in 1997. Juan Bell batted .167 with the Orioles from 1989 to 1991 (including 1 home run) and ended his career in 1995 after playing sparingly with four more teams. Brian Holton had 7 wins and 10 losses with a 4.18 era in two seasons with the Birds (1989-90). Five days after he came to the Orioles, Ken Howell was traded to the Phillies (along with pitcher Gordon Dillard) for out-fielder Phil Bradley (who was traded to the Chicago White Sox on July 30, 1990 for designated hitter/first baseman extraordinaire Ron Kittle). Bradley ended his career playing in Japan after the 1990 season.

7. **The "Where Are They Now?" Trade II.** On January 10, 1991, the Orioles traded pitchers Curt Schilling and Pete Harnisch and outfielder Steve Finley to the Houston Astros for slugging first-baseman Glenn Davis

(who had averaged 27 home runs over his previous six seasons). In 1991, Davis appeared in only 49 games for the O's and was on the disabled list from late April through late August. In 1992, on the second day of the season, he went on the DL for a month. In 1993, Davis was optioned to Rochester in May, then went on the DL from June until early September, when he was placed on waivers for the purpose of giving him his unconditional release. Meanwhile, after going from Houston to Philadelphia, Schilling won 80 game from 1992-98 and struck out 300 batters in 1997 and 1998 (and appeared in two All-Star games). Finley averaged 145 games and 25 stolen bases with the Astros and Padres from 1991-98. Harnisch had 12 wins in 1991 (and made the All-Star team) and 16 wins in 1993. Schilling, Finley and Harnisch are still in the bigs. Davis' career ended with the Orioles.

Twelve Oriole First-Round Draft Picks Who Made It With The O's (1965-98)

1.	Bobby Grich	19th overall pick in 1967
2.	Don Hood	17th pick in 1969
3.	Mike Parrott	15th pick in 1973
4.	Rich Dauer	24th pick in 1974
5.	Dave Ford	23rd pick in 1975
6.	Dallas Williams	20th pick in 1976
7.	Drungo Hazewood	19th pick in 1977
8.	Gregg Olson	4th pick in 1988
9.	Ben McDonald	1st pick in 1989
10.	Mike Mussina	20th pick in 1990
11.	Mark Smith	9th pick in 1991
12.	Jeffrey Hammonds	4th pick in 1992

Four Oriole First-Round Draft Picks Who Never Played With The O's, But Played In The Majors With Other Teams

1. Junior Kennedy (SS)   1968 draft   Reds 1974-83
2. Randy Stein (RHP)   1971 draft   Brewers, Mariners
                                           & Cubs 1978-82
3. John Hoover (RHP)   1984 draft   Rangers 1990
4. Jay Powell (RHP)   1993 draft   Marlins & Astros
                                           1995-

21 Orioles Who Were First Round Draft Picks For Other Teams

1. Mike Adamson   Phillies in 1965
2. Reggie Jackson   K.C. A's in 1966
3. Bob Reynolds   Giants in 1966
4. Don Stanhouse   A's in 1969
5. Mike Anderson   Phillies in 1969
6. Dan Ford   A's in 1970
7. Scott McGregor   Yankees in 1972
8. Jamie Quirk   Royals in 1972
9. Gary Roenicke   Expos in 1973
10. Lonnie Smith   Phillies in 1974
11. Rick Sutcliffe   Dodgers in 1974
12. Terry Kennedy   Cardinals in 1977
13. Rex Hudler   Yankees in 1978
14. Mike Morgan   A's in 1978
15. Brad Komminsk   Braves in 1979
16. Andy Van Slyke   Cardinals in 1979
17. Stan Jefferson   Mets in 1983
18. Pete Incaviglia   Expos in 1985 (did not sign)
19. Rafael Palmeiro   Cubs in 1985
20. Kevin Brown   Ranger in 1986
21. Kent Mercker   Braves in 1986

Two Orioles Who Were Number One Overall Picks For Other Teams

1. Harold Baines   White Sox in 1977
2. B.J. Surhoff   Brewers in 1985

Eight First Round Draft Picks Who Were With The Orioles in 1995

1. Harold Baines   White Sox in 1977
2. Andy Van Slyke   Cardinals in 1979
3. Rafael Palmeiro   Cubs in 1985
4. Kevin Brown   Rangers in 1986
5. Ben McDonald   Orioles in 1989
6. Mike Mussina   Orioles in 1990
7. Mark Smith   Orioles in 1991
8. Jeffrey Hammonds   Orioles in 1992

Six Orioles Draft Picks Who Didn't Sign With The Orioles—At Least Not Right Away

1. Anthony Davis   8th round 1971, 15th round 1974
   became All-American fullback at U.S.C.
2. Glenn Davis   31st in 1979
   signed with Astros, traded to O's in 1991
3. Cecil Fielder   31st in 1981
   signed with Royals, played for Blue Jays, Tigers, Angels
4. Bob Melvin   3rd in 1979
   signed with Tigers, played with O's 1989-91
5. Walt Weiss   10th in 1982
   signed with A's, 1988 A.L. Rookie of the Year
6. Dave Winfield   40th round 1969
   signed with Padres, 3,110 career hits, 465 career home runs

The All Lost-In-The-Expansion-Draft Team

RHP	Dean Chance*	1961 Los Angeles Angels
LHP	Wally Bunker	1969 Kansas City Royals
RP	Moe Drabowsky	1969 Kansas City Royals
C	Larry Haney	1969 Seattle Pilots
1B	Mike Fiore	1969 Kansas City Royals
2B	Aaron Ledesma	1998 Tampa Bay Devil Rays
SS	Bob Bailor	1977 Toronto Blue Jays
3B	Billy Klaus	1961 Washington Senators
OF	Gene Woodling	1961 Washington Senators
OF	Albie Pearson	1961 Los Angeles Angels
OF	David Dellucci	1998 Arizona Diamondbacks

Reserves

2B	Leo Burke	1961 Washington Senators
P	Mike Darr*	1977 Toronto Blue Jays
P	Bob Galasso*	1977 Seattle Mariners
C	Gene Green	1961 Washington Senators
OF	Chuck Hinton*	1961 Washington Senators
P	Richie Lewis	1993 Florida Marlins
P	Ron Moeller	1961 Los Angeles Angels
P	John Morris	1969 Seattle Pilots
P	Roger Nelson	1969 Kansas City Royals
P	Dave Pagan	1977 Seattle Mariners
IF	Don Ross*	1961 Los Angeles Angels
IF	Mike Willis*	1977 Toronto Blue Jays
P	Esteban Yan	1998 Tampa Bay Devil Rays
P	Kip Yaughn*	1993 Florida Marlins

The 1962 N.Y. Mets, 1962 Houston Colt .45s,
1969 Montreal Expos and 1969 San Diego Padres
drafted only from the National League; no Orioles
were drafted by the Colorado Rockies in 1993.

* *never appeared in a game as an Oriole*

15 • MINOR LEAGUES

Orioles Farm Teams 1954-1998

Team (State)	League (Class)	Years
Aberdeen Pheasants (SD)	Northern (C)	1954-62
Aberdeen Pheasants (SD)	Northern (A)	1963-71
Ada (OK)	Sooner State (D)	1954
Albany Polecats (GA)	South Atlantic (A)	1993-94
Amarillo Gold Sox (TX)	Texas (AA)	1959
Americus-Cordele Orioles (GA)	Georgia-Florida (D)	1955
Anderson Rebels (SC)	Tri-State (B)	1954
Appleton Foxes (WI)	Midwest (A)	1964
Asheville Orioles (NC)	Southern (AA)	1972-75
Bluefield Orioles (WV)	Appalachian (D)	1958-62
Bluefield Orioles (WV)	Appalachian (R)	1963–
Bowie Baysox (MD)	Eastern (AA)	1993–
Charlotte Knights (NC)	Southern (AA)	1987-88
Charlotte O's (NC)	Southern (AA)	1976-86
Columbus Foxes (GA)	South Atlantic (A)	1956
Cordele Orioles (GA)	Georgia-Florida (D)	1955
Dallas-Fort Worth Spurs (TX)	Texas (AA)	1969-71
Daytona Beach Admirals (FL)	Florida (A)	1985-86
Delmarva Shorebirds (MD)	South Atlantic (A)	1997–
Elmira Pioneers (NY)	New York-Penn (A)	1962
Elmira Pioneers (NY)	New York-Penn (AA)	1963-68
Erie Orioles (NY)	New York-Penn (A)	1988-89
Fayetteville Highlanders (NC)	Carolina (B)	1955
Fitzgerald Orioles (GA)	Georgia-Florida (D)	1957
Fox Cities Foxes (WS)	Three-I (B)	1960-61
Fox Cities Foxes (WS)	Midwest (A)	1963
Frederick Keys (MD)	Carolina (A)	1989–
Gulf Coast Orioles (FL)	Gulf Coast (R)	1994–
Hagerstown Suns (MD)	Carolina (A)	1982-88
Hagerstown Suns (MD)	Eastern (AA)	1989-92
High Desert Mavericks (CA)	California (A)	1995-96
Knoxville Smokies (TN)	South Atlantic (A)	1957-58
Kane County Cougars (IL)	Midwest (A)	1991-92

Leesburg Orioles (FL)	Florida (D)	1960-61
Lewiston Broncs (ID)	Western Int'l. (A)	1954
Lewiston Broncs (ID)	Pioneer (A)	1972
Little Rock Travelers (AR)	Southern Assoc. (AA)	1961
Lodi Orioles (CA)	California (A)	1974
Lodi Orions (CA)	California (A)	1972
Lodi Lions (CA)	California (A)	1973
Louisville Colonels (KY)	American Assoc. (AAA)	1958
Lubbock Hubbers (TX)	Big State (B)	1956
Marion Marauders (NC)	Tar Heel (D)	1954
Miami Marlins (FL)	International (AAA)	1959-60
Miami Marlins (FL)	Florida State (A)	1966-70
Miami Orioles (FL)	Florida State (A)	1971-81
Newark Orioles (NY)	New York-Penn (A)	1983-87
Paris Orioles (TX)	Sooner State (D)	1955-57
Pensacola Dons (FL)	Ala.-Fla. (D)	1958-59
Phoenix Stars (AZ)	Ariz.-Mex. (C)	1956-57
Pine Bluff Judges (AR)	Cotton States (C)	1954
Rochester Red Wings (NY)	International (AAA)	1961–
San Antonio Missions (TX)	Texas (AA)	1954-57
San Jose Bees (CA)	California (A)	1983
Sarasota Orioles (FL)	Gulf Coast (R)	1991-93
Stockton Ports (CA)	California (C)	1959-62
Stockton Ports (CA)	California (A)	1963-71
Thetford Mines Miners (QUE)	Provincial (C)	1954
Thomson Orioles (GA)	Georgia State (D)	1956
Tri-City (WA)	Northwest (B)	1961
Tri-City (WA)	Northwest (A)	1965
Vancouver Mounties (BC)	Pacific Coast (Open)	1956-57
Vancouver Mounties (BC)	Pacific Coast (AAA)	1958-60
Victoria Rosebuds (TX)	Texas (AA)	1961
Wausau Timbers (WI)	Midwest (A)	1990
Wichita Indians (KS)	Western (A)	1954-55
Wilson Tobacconists (NC)	Carolina (B)	1958
Wytheville Statesman (VA)	Appalachian (D)	1954
York White Roses (PA)	Piedmont (B)	1954-55

Eight Orioles Who Were International League MVPs With The Rochester Red Wings

1. Mike Epstein	1966	
2. Merv Rettenmund	1968	
3. Roger Freed	1970	
4. Bob Grich	1971	
5. Jim Fuller	1973	
6. Rich Dauer	1976 (Co-winner)	
7. Craig Worthington	1988	
8. Jeff Manto	1994	

Ten Orioles Who Were International League Rookie Of The Year With The Rochester Red Wings

1. Mike Epstein	1966
2. Curt Motton	1967
3. Merv Rettenmund	1968
4. Roger Freed	1970
5. Al Bumbry	1972
6. Rich Dauer	1976
7. Bob Bonner	1980
8. Cal Ripken, Jr.	1981
9. Steve Finley	1988
10. Luis Mercedes	1991

Five Orioles Who Were International League Most Valuable Pitcher With The Rochester Red Wings

1. Dave Leonhard   1967
2. Roric Harrison   1971
3. Dennis Martinez   1976
4. Mike Parrott   1977
5. Mike Mussina   1991

Five Orioles Who Were International League Batting Leaders With The Rochester Red Wings

1. Merv Rettenmund   .331 in 1968
2. Bobby Grich   .336 in 1971
3. Al Bumbry   .345 in 1972
4. Rich Dauer   .336 in 1976
5. Steve Finley   .314 in 1988

Seven Orioles Who Were International League Home Run Leaders With The Rochester Red Wings

1. Boog Powell   29 in 1961
2. Mike Epstein   29 in 1966
3. Bobby Grich   32 in 1971
4. Jim Fuller   39 in 1973
5. Terry Crowley   30 in 1977
6. Ken Gerhart   28 in 1986
7. Jeff Manto   31 in 1994

Eleven Orioles Who Won Other Minor League Awards

1. Fred Valentine	1958 Carolina League MVP
2. Mike Epstein	1965 California League MVP
3. Bob Grich	1969 Texas League MVP
4. Enos Cabell	1971 Texas League MVP
5. Jim Fuller	1971 Florida State League MVP
6. Mike Reinbach	1972 Southern League MVP
7. Eddie Murray	1973 Appalachian League Rookie of the Year
8. Dan Graham	1976 California League MVP and Rookie of the Year (while with Twins organization)
9. Mark Corey	1976 Appalachian League MVP
10. Jeff Manto	1988 Texas League MVP (while with Indians organization)
11. Calvin Pickering	1998 Eastern League Player of the Year

Seven Orioles Who Were Voted Minor League Player of the Year

1. Norm Siebern	1957 (with Yankees organization)
2. Don Buford	1963 (with White Sox organization)
3. Mike Epstein	1966
4. Merv Rettenmund	1968
5. Don Baylor	1970
6. Bob Grich	1971
7. Mike Reinbach	1972

Two Oriole Pitchers Who Led The Minor Leagues In Won-Lost Percentage

1. Jerry Walker   .818 with Knoxville in 1958
2. Eddie Watt   .895 with Aberdeen
                       and Elmira in 1964

Four Orioles Who Led The Minor Leagues In Batting

1. George Kell   .396 with Lancaster in 1943
2. Russ Snyder   .432 with McAlester in 1953
3. Chico Garcia   .368 with Monterrey in 1963
4. Nelson Simmons   .382 with Jalisco in 1993

25 Teams Named "Orioles" NOT From Baltimore

Baltimore Orioles' farm teams in italics

1. *Americus-Cordele, GA*	*Georgia-Florida League, 1954*
2. *Asheville, NC*	*Southern League, 1972-75*
3. *Bluefield, WV*	*Appalachian League, 1958-present*
4. Centreville, MD	Eastern Shore League, 1946
5. *Cordele, GA*	*Georgia-Florida League, 1955*
6. Dover, DE	Eastern Shore League, 1937-40
7. Dublin, GA	Georgia-Florida League, 1958
8. *Erie, PA*	*New York-Penn League, 1988-89*
9. *Fitzgerald, GA*	*Georgia-Florida League, 1957*
10. *Gulf Coast, FL*	*Gulf Coast League, 1990-present*
11. Kingsport, TN	Appalachian League, 1957
12. Lawrence, KS	Kansas-Missouri League, 1892
13. Leavenworth, KS	Missouri Valley League, 1904

14. Leavenworth, KS	Western Association, 1905
15. Leesburg, FL	*Florida State League, 1960-61*
16. Lodi, CA	*California League, 1974-75*
17. Miami, FL	*Florida State League, 1971-81*
18. Newark, NY	*New York-Penn League, 1983-87*
19. Ontario, Canada	Sunset League, 1947
20. Paris, TX	*Sooner State League, 1955-57*
21. Springfield, MO	Western Association, 1920
22. Tarboro, NC	Coastal Plain League, 1941
23. Thomasville, GA	Georgia-Florida League, 1935-39
24. Thomasville, NC	North Carolina State League, 1938
25. Thomson, GA	*Georgia State League, 1956*

47 Maryland Minor League Teams

1. Baltimore	Eastern League, 1884
2. Baltimore Orioles	Atlantic Association, 1890
3. Baltimore Orioles	Eastern League, 1903-14
4. Baltimore Orioles	International League, 1916-53
5. Bowie Baysox	Eastern League, 1993-present
6. Cambridge Canners	Eastern Shore League, 1922-28
7. Cambridge Cardinals	Eastern Shore League, 1937-41
8. Cambridge Dodgers	Eastern Shore League, 1946-49
9. Centreville Colts	Eastern Shore League, 1937
10. Centreville Red Sox	Eastern Shore League, 1939-41
11. Crisfield Crabbers	Eastern Shore League, 1922-28, 1937
12. Cumberland	POM League, 1906
13. Cumberland Rooters	Western Pennsylvania League, 1907

14. Cumberland Colts	Blue Ridge League, 1917
15. Cumberland Colts	Mid-Atlantic League, 1925-32
16. Delmarva Shorebirds	South Atlantic League, 1996-present
17. Easton Farmers	Eastern Shore League, 1924-28
18. Easton Browns	Eastern Shore League, 1937
19. Easton Cubs	Eastern Shore League, 1938
20. Easton Yankees	Eastern Shore League, 1939-41, 1946-49
21. Federalsburg Little A's	Eastern Shore League, 1937-41
22. Federalsburg A's	Eastern Shore League, 1946-48
23. Federalsburg Feds	Eastern Shore League, 1949
24. Frederick Hustlers	Blue Ridge League, 1915-17, 1920-28
25. Frederick Warriors	Blue Ridge League, 1929-30
26. Frederick Keys	Carolina League, 1989-present
27. Frostburg Demons	Potomac League, 1916
28. Hagerstown	Cumberland Valley League, 1896
29. Hagerstown Blues	Blue Ridge League, 1915
30. Hagerstown Hubs	Blue Ridge League, 1916, 1924-31
31. Hagerstown Terriers	Blue Ridge League, 1917, 1923
32. Hagerstown Champs	Blue Ridge League, 1920-22
33. Hagerstown Owls	Inter-State League, 1941-49
34. Hagerstown Braves	Inter-State League, 1950-51
35. Hagerstown Braves	Piedmont League, 1953
36. Hagerstown Packets	Piedmont League, 1954-55
37. Hagerstown Suns	Carolina League, 1981-88
38. Hagerstown Suns	Eastern League, 1989-present
39. Lonacoming Giants	Potomac League, 1916
40. Pocomoke City Chicks	Eastern Shore League, 1940

41. Pocomoke City Salamanders	Eastern Shore League, 1922
42. Pocomoke City Red Sox	Eastern Shore League, 1937-39
43. Queen Anne Colts	Eastern Shore League, 1938
44. Salisbury Indians	Eastern Shore League, 1922-28, 1937
45. Salisbury Cardinals	Eastern Shore League, 1938-41, 1946-49
46. Salisbury A's	Inter-State League, 1951
47. Salisbury Reds	Inter-State League, 1952

16 • OTHER TEAMS

The Ones-That-Got-Away Team
(players whose fortunes improved after they left Baltimore)

SP	Dennis Martinez (Expos, Indians, Mariners, Braves)
RP	Jose Mesa (Indians)
C	Mickey Tettleton (Tigers & Rangers)
1B	Don Baylor (Angels)
2B	Bobby Grich (Angels)
SS	*(it seems that the O's haven't let any get away)*
3B	Doug DeCinces (Angels)
OF	Reggie Jackson (Yankees & Angels)
OF	Lou Piniella (Royals & Yankees)
OF	Steve Finley (Astros & Padres)

Nine Future Orioles Who Made Their Major League Debut From April 15 To April 20, 1952

1. Jim Fridley   April 15 with the Indians
2. Johnny Temple   April 15 with the Reds
3. Billy Klaus   April 16 with the Boston Braves
4. Gene Stephens   April 16 with the Red Sox
5. Ike Delock   April 17 with the Red Sox
6. Billy Hoeft   April 18 with the Tigers
7. Hoyt Wilhelm   April 19 with the New York Giants
8. Darrell Johnson   April 20 with the St. Louis Browns
9. Bill Miller   April 20 with the Yankees

Three Who Made Their Major League Debut With The Orioles And Were Later All-Stars With The California Angels

1. Don Baylor
2. Doug DeCinces
3. Bobby Grich

Two Orioles In The Baseball Hall Of Fame Who Made Their Major League Debut On April 17, 1956

1. Luis Aparicio (White Sox)
2. Frank Robinson (Reds)

Note: On the same day, Tito Francona debuted with the Orioles, and Whitey Herzog debuted with the Senators.

Orioles Who Made Their Major League Debut On The Same Day, For The Same Team, But Not The O's

1. Bobby Adams and Grady Hatton (Reds)	April 16, 1946
2. Harry Dorish and Sam Mele (Red Sox)	April 15, 1947
3. Bob Chakales and George Zuverink (Indians)	April 21, 1951
4. Jim Brideweser and Clint Courtney (Yankees)	September 29, 1951
5. Frank Kellert and Don Larsen (Browns)	April 18, 1953
6. Kevin Bass and Doug Jones (Brewers)	April 9, 1982
7. Phil Bradley and Harold Reynolds (Mariners)	September 2, 1983

Two Oriole DHs Named Tommy Who Wore Number 12 And Played For The 1969 Seattle Pilots

1. Tommy Davis
2. Tommy Harper

Three Orioles Who Pitched A Shutout In Their First Major League Start (Though Not As An Oriole)

1. Mike Fornieles	June 10, 1950 with the Senators
2. Stu Miller	August 12, 1952 with the Cardinals
3. Fernando Valenzuela	April 9, 1981 with the Dodgers

Four Orioles Who Hit Home Runs From Both Sides Of The Plate In The Same Game (Though Not With The Orioles)

1. Bobby Bonilla	July 3, 1987 with the Pirates
	April 6, 1988 with the Pirates
2. Kevin Bass	August 3, 1987 with the Astros
	September 2, 1987 with the Astros
	August 20, 1989 with the Astros
	August 2, 1992 with the Giants
3. Eddie Murray	April 18, 1990 with the Dodgers
	June 9, 1990 with the Dodgers
4. Bret Barberie	August 2, 1991 with the Expos

Three Orioles Whose Numbers Were Retired By Other Teams

1. Harold Baines	Number 3	White Sox
2. Luis Aparicio	Number 11	White Sox
3. Robin Roberts	Number 36	Phillies

The All-Made-Their-Major-League-Debut-With-The-Tigers Team

SP	Dizzy Trout	305 starts with Tigers
RP	Pat Dobson	104 games with Tigers
C	Joe Ginsberg	253 games at C
1B	Jim Northrup	34 games at 1B (1,190 in OF)
2B	Tom Matchick	60 games at 2B
SS	Neil Berry	161 games at SS
3B	Elliott Maddox	40 games at 3B
OF	Hoot Evers	708 games in OF
OF	Vic Wertz	691 games in OF
OF	Fred Lynn	22 games in OF
DH	Nelson Simmons	35 games at DH

Eight Long-Time Orioles Who Ended Their Careers with Other Teams (And Their Post-Oriole Stats)

1. Mark Belanger   Dodgers 1982
(54 games, 240 avg., 0 HR)

2. Paul Blair   Yankees 1977-79, 1980; Reds 1979
(160 games, .240 avg., 5 HR)

3. Al Bumbry   Padres 1985
(68 games, .200 avg., 1 HR)

4. Mike Cuellar   Angels 1977
(2 games, 0W-1L, 21.00 ERA)

5. Tippy Martinez   Twins 1988
(3 games, 0W-0L, 18.00 ERA)

6. Dave McNally   Expos 1975
(12 games, 3W-6L, 5.26 ERA)

7. Boog Powell   Indians 1975-76; Dodgers 1977
(287 games, .263 avg., 36 HR)

8. Eddie Watt   Phillies 1974, Cubs 1975
(48 games, 1W-2L)

Highs And Lows With Oriole Catcher Joe Ginsberg

1. Joe played in 3 games with the 1954 Cleveland Indians who are second in the A.L. in wins in a season (111).
2. Joe ended his 13-year career by playing in 2 games for the 1962 New York Mets who are second in the majors in losses in a season (120).

The All-Made-Their-Major-League-Debut-With-The-Reds Team

SP	Howie Fox	121 starts with Reds
RP	Norm Charlton	238 appearances with Reds
C	Dave Van Gorder	164 games at C
1B	Lee May	671 games at 1B
2B	Johnny Temple	948 games at 2B
SS	Wade Rowdon	7 games at SS
3B	Chris Sabo	749 games at 3B
OF	Frank Robinson	1,278 games in OF
OF	Eric Davis	931 games in OF
OF	Tommy Harper	616 games in OF

Four Orioles Who Played At Least 500 Games At Third Base For The Cincinnati Reds

1. Chris Sabo   749 games
2. Grady Hatton   729 games
3. Bobby Adams   565 games
4. Ray Knight   527 games

Seven Now Defunct Teams That Oriole George Brunet Pitched For

1. Kansas City Athletics   1956-60
2. Milwaukee Braves   1960-61
3. Houston Colt .45s   1962-63
4. Los Angeles Angels   1964
5. California Angels   1965-69
6. Seattle Pilots   1969
7. Washington Senators   1970

Three Orioles Who Were World Series MVPs For The New York Yankees

1. Reggie Jackson   1977
2. Don Larsen   1956
3. Bob Turley   1958

The All-Played-For-The-Old-Washington-Senators (Who Moved To Minnesota In 1961) Team

SP	Dean Stone	69 games started
RP	Dick Hyde	152 relief appearances
C	Clint Courtney	383 game at C
1B	Eddie Robinson	179 games at 1B
2B	Billy Gardner	145 games at 2B
SS	Billy Klaus	18 games at SS
3B	Bob Johnson	74 games at 3B
OF	Gil Coan	630 games in OF
OF	Jim Busby	480 games in OF
OF	Sam Mele	293 in OF

The All-Played-For-The-New-Washington-Senators (Who Moved To Texas In 1972) Team

SP	Pete Richert	73 games started
RP	Darold Knowles	297 relief appearances
C	Hobie Landrith	37 games at C
1B	Mike Epstein	454 games at 1B
2B	Bob Saverine	118 games at 118
SS	Ron Hansen	81 games at SS
3B	Aurelio Rodriguez	136 games at 3B
OF	Fred Valentine	369 games in OF
OF	Willie Kirkland	187 games in OF
OF	Willie Tasby	149 games in OF

Eight Teams Where At Least 10% Of Oriole Players Have Played (Out Of A Total Of 633 Orioles From 1954 Through 1998)

1. Cleveland Indians	16.9% (109 players)
2. Chicago White Sox	15.6% (99 players)
3. New York Yankees	15% (95 players)
4. Detroit Tigers	12.9% (82 players)
5. Philadelphia Phillies	12.3% (78 players)
6. St. Louis Cardinals	11.8% (75 players)
7. Cincinnati Reds	11.8% (75 players)
8. Boston Red Sox	11.2% (71 players)

Eight Teams Where At Least 20 Orioles Made Their Major League Debut

1. New York Yankees	27
2. Cincinnati Reds	24
3. Chicago White Sox	23
4. Detroit Tigers	22
5. Boston Red Sox	21
6. Cleveland Indians	21
7. Philadelphia Phillies	21
8. St. Louis Cardinals	20

Two World Championship Teams Since 1950 That Had No Former Or Future Orioles

1. 1969 New York Mets
2. 1976 Cincinnati Reds

The All-Made-Their-Major-League-Debut-With-The-Cardinals Team

SP	Harvey Haddix	108 starts with Cardinals
RP	Nelson Briles	116 games with Cardinals
C	Del Rice	1,017 games at C
1B	Jim Dwyer	3 games at 1B
2B	*no Oriole ever played 2B for the Cardinals*	
SS	Kelly Paris	4 games at SS
3B	Todd Zeile	635 games at 3B
OF	Tito Landrum	419 games in OF
OF	Andy Van Slyke	402 games in OF
OF	Chuck Diering	329 games in OF

Six Former Or Future Orioles Who Played With The A's Against The O's In The 1971 ALCS

1. Curt Blefary
2. Tommy Davis
3. Dave Duncan
4. Mike Epstein
5. Reggie Jackson
6. Darold Knowles

Six Former Or Future Orioles Who Played With The Angel's Against The O's In The 1979 ALCS

1. Don Aase
2. Don Baylor
3. Dan Ford
4. Bobby Grich
5. Larry Harlow
6. Merv Rettenmund

Six Former Or Future Oriole Pitchers Who Won Games Against The O's In The Post Season

1.	Nelson Briles (Pirates)	1 W, 1971 World Series
2.	Ken Holtzman (A's)	2 W, 1973 & 1974 ALCS
3.	Don Aase (Angels)	1 W, 1979 ALCS
4.	Grant Jackson (Pirates)	1 W, 1979 World Series
5.	Jimmy Key (Yankees)	1 W, 1996 ALCS
6.	Jose Mesa (Indians)	1 W, 1997 ALCS

Four Former Or Future Orioles To Homer Against The O's In The Post Season

1.	Lee May (Reds)	2 HR, 1970 World Series
2.	Reggie Jackson (A's)	2 HR, 1971 ALCS
3.	Don Baylor (Angels)	1 HR, 1979 ALCS
4.	Dan Ford (Angels)	2 HR, 1979 ALCS

The All-Made-Their-Major-League-Debut-With-The-Yankees Team

SP	Scott Kamieniecki	94 games started
RP	Tippy Martinez	42 relief appearances
C	Gus Triandos	24 games at C
1B	Dick Kryhoski	51 games at 1B
2B	Rex Hudler	25 games at 2B
SS	Frank Baker	73 games at SS
3B	Mike Pagliarulo	684 games at 3B
OF	Norm Siebern	277 games in OF
OF	Tom Shopay	18 games in OF
OF	Marv Throneberry	18 games in OF

Two Orioles Who Played For Both The New York Yankees And The New York Giants

1. Billy Gardner
2. Mike McCormick

Six Orioles Who Played For Both The New York Yankees And The New York Mets

1. Keith Hughes
2. Stan Jefferson
3. Elliott Maddox
4. Bill Short
5. Marv Throneberry
6. Gene Woodling

Two Orioles Who Played For Both the Boston Red Sox And the Boston Braves

1. Billy Klaus
2. Jim Wilson

Ten Orioles Who Played For Both the Chicago White Sox And The Chicago Cubs

1. John Buzhardt
2. Tommy Davis
3. Moe Drabowsky
4. Don Larsen
5. Dick Littlefield
6. Morrie Martin
7. Bob Molinaro
8. Tim Stoddard
9. Steve Stone
10. Hoyt Wilhelm

One Oriole Who Played For Both The Philadelphia Phillies And The Philadelphia A's

1. Dave Philley (of course!)

The All-Made-Their-Major-League-Debut-With-The-Phillies Team

SP	Robin Roberts	472 starts with Phillies
RP	Grant Jackson	84 games with Phillies
C	Clay Dalrymple	944 games at C
1B	Francisco Melendez	12 games at 1B
2B	Steve Scarsone	3 games at 2B
SS	Shane Turner	5 games at SS
3B	Rick Schu	229 games at 3B
OF	Mike Anderson	365 games in OF
OF	Jeff Stone	199 games in OF
OF	Lonnie Smith	155 games in OF

Some Non-Oriole Firsts

1. Clint Courtney is the first catcher to wear glasses (while with the St. Louis Browns) in 1952.
2. Don Larsen pitches the first (and only) World Series perfect game on October 8, 1956 (for the Yankees).
3. Frank Robinson becomes the first black manager in the major leagues with Cleveland in 1975.

Four Orioles Who Were All-Stars Before And After Their Stint With The Orioles, But Not During

1. Kevin Brown	Rangers 1992
	Marlins 1996-97
	Padres 1998
2. Reggie Jackson	A's 1969, 1971-1975
	Yankees 1977, 1979-81
	Angels 1982, 1984
3. Vic Wertz	Tigers 1949, 1951-52
	Indians 1957
4. David Wells	Tigers 1985
	Yankees 1998

The All-Made-Their-Major-League-Debut-With-The-Red Sox Team

SP	Ike Delock	142 starts with Bosox
RP	Tom Bolton	67 games with Bosox
C	Ernie Whitt	8 games at C
1B	Walt Dropo	182 games at 1B
2B	Billy Goodman	527 games at 2B
SS	Rick Burleson	1,004 games at SS
3B	Juan Beniquez	14 games at 3B
OF	Dwight Evans	2,079 games in OF
OF	Fred Lynn	811 games in OF
OF	Gene Stephens	547 games in OF
DH	Sam Horn	70 games at DH

Three Orioles Who Were All-Star Shortstops For The Boston Red Sox

1. Luis Aparicio   1971
2. Rick Burleson   1977, 1979
3. Vern Stephens   1948-51

Six Orioles Who Were All-Star Pitchers For The Detroit Tigers

1. Doyle Alexander   1988
2. Ted Gray   1950
3. Billy Hoeft   1955
4. Art Houtteman   1950
5. Dizzy Trout   1944, 1947
6. David Wells   1995

Five Orioles Who Were All-Star Pitchers For The New York Yankees

1. Ryne Duren   1958-59, 1961
2. Jimmy Key   1993-94
3. Eddie Lopat   1951
4. Bob Turley   1955, 1958
5. David Wells   1998

Four Orioles Who Were All-Star Pitchers For The Chicago White Sox

1. Sandy Consuegra 1954
2. Ed Farmer   1980
3. Eddie Fisher   1965
4. Jim Wilson   1956

Five Orioles Who Were All-Star Outfielders For The Chicago White Sox

1.	Harold Baines	1985-87
2.	Jim Busby	1951
3.	Pat Kelly	1973
4.	Ron Kittle	1983
5.	Al Smith	1955

Three Orioles Who Were All-Star Shortstops For The Chicago White Sox

1.	Chico Carrasquel	1951, 1953-55
2.	Luis Aparicio	1958-62, 1970
3.	Ozzie Guillen	1990-91

The All-Made-Their-Major-League-Debut-With-The-White Sox Team

SP	Eddie Lopat	109 starts with Chisox
RP	Kevin Hickey	124 games with Chisox
C	Camilo Carreon	298 games at C
1B	Greg Walker	689 games at 1B
2B	Don Buford	321 games at 2B
SS	Luis Aparicio	1,491 games at SS
3B	Bob Kennedy	414 games at 3B
OF	Dave Philley	629 games in OF
OF	Ron Kittle	458 games in OF
OF	Jim Busby	266 games in OF
DH	Harold Baines	481 games at DH

Nine Orioles Who Played For The 1952 World Champion New York Yankees

1. Jim Brideweser
2. Bob Kuzava
3. Eddie Lopat
4. Jim McDonald
5. Bill Miller
6. Art Schallock
7. Johnny Schmitz
8. Kal Segrist
9. Gene Woodling

Plus Orioles Manager Hank Bauer and Orioles Coach Ray Scarborough

Ten Orioles Who Played For The 1953 World Champion New York Yankees

1. Jim Brideweser
2. Bob Kuzava
3. Eddie Lopat
4. Jim McDonald
5. Bill Miller
6. Willie Miranda
7. Art Schallock
8. Johnny Schmitz
9. Gus Triandos
10. Gene Woodling

Plus Orioles Manager Hank Bauer and Orioles Coach Ray Scarborough

Eight Orioles Who Played For The 1972 World Champion Oakland Athletics

1. Curt Blefary
2. Larry Brown
3. Dave Duncan
4. Mike Epstein
5. Larry Haney
6. Ken Holtzman
7. Reggie Jackson
8. Darold Knowles

Plus the A's were managed by former Oriole Dick Williams.

Eight Orioles Who Played For The 1986 World Champion New York Mets

1. Sid Fernandez
2. Stan Jefferson
3. Ray Knight
4. Roger McDowell
5. John Mitchell
6. Randy Myers
7. Jesse Orosco
8. Doug Sisk

Plus the 1986 Mets were managed by Davey Johnson.

The All-Played-For-The-New-York-Giants Team

SP	Dave Koslo	188 starts with the Giants
RP	Hoyt Wilhelm	319 relief appearances
C	Valmy Thomas	88 games at C
1B	Whitey Lockman	613 games at 1B
2B	Billy Gardner	17 games at 2B
SS	Foster Castleman	3 games at SS
3B	Ozzie Virgil	69 games at 3B
OF	Bobby Thomson	851 games in OF
OF	Jackie Brandt	96 games in OF
OF	Chuck Diering	36 games in the OF

Five Orioles Who Had Great Post-Season Moments—for Other Teams

1. Bobby Thomson (Orioles 1960) hit baseball's famous "shot heard round the world," the game–ending home run that clinched the 1951 National League pennant for the New York Giants in a one–game playoff against the Brooklyn Dodgers.

2. Don Larsen (Orioles 1954 and 1965) pitched the only perfect game in World Series history, for the New York Yankees in Game Five of the 1956 Fall Classic—after being shelled in the second game of that Series.

3. Reggie Jackson (Orioles 1976) earned the nickname "Mr. October" for his outstanding World Series performances for the 1973 Oakland A's and the 1977–78 New York Yankees. In '73 and '77, Jackson won the series MVP crown. His greatest post-season triumph came when he collected three home runs in the sixth and deciding game of the 1977 series against the Los Angeles Dodgers.

4. Ray Knight (Orioles 1987) was the World Series MVP for the 1986 Mets in their dramatic seven-game victory over the Boston Red Sox. Knight batted .391 and scored the winning run in a come-from-behind Game Six victory, on grounder bobbled by Boston first baseman Bill Buckner after it appeared that the Sox had the Series wrapped up. (Jesse Orosco was the winning pitcher.)

5. Joe Carter (Orioles 1998) hit the series-ending home run for the Toronto Blue Jays off of reliever Mitch Williams to beat the Philadelphia Phillies in the 1993 World Series.

The All-Made-Their-Major-League-Debut-With-The-Indians Team

SP	Roy Smith	25 starts with Indians
RP	Ed Farmer	100 games with Indians
C	Dick Brown	143 games at C
1B	Eddie Robinson	234 games at 1B
2B	Bobby Avila	1,098 games at 2B
SS	Larry Brown	680 games at SS
3B	Jeff Manto	45 games at 3B
OF	Al Smith	448 games in OF
OF	John Lowenstein	365 games in OF
OF	Jim Fridley	54 games in OF

19 Orioles Who Won
Major Awards For Other Teams

1. Luis Aparicio	1956 Rookie of the Year, White Sox
2. Don Baylor	1979 MVP, Angels
3. Doug Drabek	1990 Cy Young, Pirates
4. Walt Dropo	1950 Rookie of the Year, Red Sox
5. Reggie Jackson	1973 MVP, A's
	1973 World Series MVP, A's
	1977 World Series MVP, Yankees
6. Ron Kittle	1983 Rookie of the Year, White Sox
7. Ray Knight	1986 World Series MVP, Mets
8. Don Larsen	1956 World Series MVP, Yankees
9. Fred Lynn	1975 Rookie of the Year, Red Sox
	1975 MVP, Red Sox
	1982 ALCS MVP, Angels
	1983 All-Star Game MVP, Angels
10. Mike McCormick	1967 Cy Young, Giants
11. Albie Pearson	1958 Rookie of the Year, Senators
12. Lou Piniella	1969 Rookie of the Year, Royals
13. Frank Robinson	1956 Rookie of the Year, Reds
	1961 MVP, Reds
14. Chris Sabo	1988 Rookie of the Year, Reds
15. Rick Sutcliffe	1979 Rookie of the Year, Dodgers
	1984 Cy Young, Cubs
16. Bob Turley	1958 Cy Young, Yankees
	1958 World Series MVP, Yankees
17. Fernando Valenzuela	1981 Rookie of the Year, Dodgers
	1981 Cy Young, Dodgers
18. Jerome Walton	1989 Rookie of the Year, Cubs
19. Earl Williams	1971 Rookie of the Year, Braves

Nine Other Teams Named
The Baltimore Orioles

1. American Association, 1883-89 – had been the Lord Baltimores in 1882.
2. Atlantic Association, 1890 – disbanded after 1890 season.
3. National League, 1892-99 – disbanded after 1899 season, but not before winning three straight National League pennants from 1894 to 1896; team included such future Hall of Famers as Willie Keeler, Hughie Jennings, John McGraw and Wilbert Robinson.
4. American League, 1901-02 – became the New York Highlanders in 1903 (and eventually the New York Yankees—feh!).
5. Eastern League (A), 1903-07.
6. Eastern League (AA), 1908-11.
7. International League (AA), 1912-14 – became the Richmond Climbers in 1915; Babe Ruth played for this team.
8. International League (AA), 1916-45 – team included future Hall of Famer and Maryland native Lefty Grove.
9. International League (AAA), 1946-53 – disbanded after 1953 season to make room for our current American League Baltimore Orioles.

And 13 More Baltimore Baseball Teams

1. Baltimore, Eastern League, 1884 – became the Lancaster Lancasters in mid-1884.
2. Baltimore Black Sox, Eastern Colored League, 1923-1928 – disbanded during 1928 season.
3. Baltimore Black Sox, American Negro League, 1929 – disbanded during 1929 season.
4. Baltimore Black Sox, East-West League, 1932 – disbanded during 1932 season.
5. Baltimore Black Sox, Negro National League, 1933-34 – disbanded after 1934 season.
6. Baltimore Elite Giants, Negro National League, 1938-48 – had been the Washington Elite Giants.
7. Baltimore Elite Giants, Negro American League, 1949-50 – disbanded after 1950 season.
8. Baltimore Lord Baltimores, National Association, 1872-74 – also known as the Baltimore Marylands during the 1873 season; disbanded after 1874 season.
9. Baltimore Monumentals, Union Association, 1884 – became the Lancaster Ironsides during the 1884 season.
10. Baltimore Terrapins, Federal League, 1914-15 – also known as the Baltimore Baltfeds; disbanded after 1915 season.
11. Lord Baltimores, National Association, 1872 – renamed Maryland of Baltimore in 1873.
12. Lord Baltimores, American Association, 1882 – became Baltimore Orioles in 1883.
13. Maryland Of Baltimore, National Association, 1873-74 – disbanded after 1874 season.

17 • THE ALPHABET TEAMS

Player must have played in at least one game at a particular position as an Oriole.

The A Team

MGR	Joe Altobelli
COA	Luke Appling
SP	Doyle Alexander
RP	Don Aase
C	Andy Etchebarren
	(so, I cheated a little!)
1B	Cal Abrams
2B	Roberto Alomar
SS	Luis Aparicio
3B	Jerry Adair
OF	Brady Anderson
OF	Cal Abrams
OF	Mike Anderson
DH	Benny Ayala

The All-C Team

SP	Mike Cuellar
RP	Terry Clark
C	Clint Courtney
1B	Enos Cabell
2B	Wayne Causey
SS	Chico Carrasquel
3B	Todd Cruz
OF	Rich Coggins
OF	Gil Coan
OF	Joe Carter
DH	Terry Crowley

The All-B Team

MGR	Hank Bauer
COA	Harry Brecheen
SP	Steve Barber
RP	Armando Benitez
C	Dick Brown
1B	Bob Boyd
2B	Don Buford
SS	Mark Belanger
3B	Bobby Bonilla
OF	Paul Blair
OF	Al Bumbry
OF	Don Baylor
DH	Harold Baines

The All-D Team

SP	Pat Dobson
RP	Moe Drabowsky
C	Rick Dempsey
1B	Glenn Davis
2B	Rich Dauer
SS	Jerry DaVanon
3B	Doug DeCinces
OF	Mike Devereaux
OF	Eric Davis
OF	Chuck Diering
DH	Tommy Davis

The All-F Team

SP	Mike Flanagan
RP	Todd Frohwirth
C	Hank Foiles
1B	Tito Francona
2B	P.J Forbes
SS	Bobby Floyd
3B	Jim Finigan
OF	Dan Ford
OF	Steve Finley
OF	Jim Fridley
DH	Jim Fuller

The All-H Team

MGR	Billy Hitchcock
COA	Billy Hunter
SP	Jim Hardin
RP	Dick Hall
C	Elrod Hendricks
1B	Bob Hale
2B	Tim Hulett
SS	Ron Hansen
3B	Leo Hernandez
OF	Jeffrey Hammonds
OF	Larry Harlow
OF	Whitey Herzog
DH	Sam Horn

The All-G Team

SP	Ross Grimsley
RP	Mike Griffin
C	Joe Ginsberg
1B	Jim Gentile
2B	Billy Gardner
SS	Bobby Grich
3B	Rene Gonzales
OF	Ken Gerhart
OF	Joe Gaines
OF	Lenny Green
DH	Leo Gomez

The All-J Team

MGR	Davey Johnson
COA	Al Jackson
SP	Dave Johnson
RP	Grant Jackson
C	Darrell Johnson
1B	Bob Johnson
2B	Ricky Jones
SS	Davey Johnson
3B	Ron Jackson
OF	Reggie Jackson
OF	Stan Jefferson
OF	Lou Jackson

The Special-K Team

SP	Jimmy Key
RP	Darold Knowles
C	Terry Kennedy
1B	Frank Kellert
2B	Billy Klaus
SS	Wayne Krenchicki
3B	George Kell
OF	Pat Kelly
OF	Willie Kirkland
OF	Brad Komminsk
DH	Ron Kittle

The All-M Team

SP	Dave McNally
RP	Stu Miller
C	Bob Melvin
1B	Eddie Murray
2B	Mark McLemore
SS	Willie Miranda
3B	Jeff Manto
OF	Curt Motton
OF	Dave May
OF	Andres Mora
DH	Lee May

The All-L Team

SP	Don Larsen
RP	Dave Leonhard
C	Charlie Lau
1B	Whitey Lockman
2B	Don Leppert
SS	Aaron Ledesma
3B	John Lowenstein
OF	Fred Lynn
OF	Lee Lacy
OF	Tito Landrum
DH	Carlos Lopez

The All-P Team

SP	Jim Palmer
RP	Jim Poole
C	Mark Parent
1B	Rafael Palmeiro
2B	Kelly Paris
SS	Buddy Peterson
3B	Mike Pagliarulo
OF	Boog Powell
OF	Al Pilarcik
OF	Dave Philley
DH	Luis Polonia

The All-R Team

MGR	Paul Richards
COA	Cal Ripken, Sr.
SP	Robin Roberts
RP	Pete Richert
C	Floyd Rayford
1B	Eddie Robinson
2B	Bill Ripken
SS	Cal Ripken, Jr.
3B	Brooks Robinson
OF	Frank Robinson
OF	Merv Rettenmund
OF	Earl Robinson
DH	Vic Rodriguez

The All-T Team

SP	Mike Torrez
RP	Anthony Telford
C	Gus Triandos
1B	Marv Throneberry
2B	Johnny Temple
SS	Tim Hulett
	(so I cheated again!)
3B	Jeff Tackett
OF	Willie Tasby
OF	Mickey Tettleton
OF	Tony Tarasco
DH	Jim Traber

The All-S Team

SP	Rick Sutcliffe
RP	Don Stanhouse
C	Dave Skaggs
1B	Norm Siebern
2B	Billy Smith
SS	Lenn Sakata
3B	Vern Stephens
OF	Ken Singleton
OF	Russ Snyder
OF	B.J. Surhoff
DH	Larry Sheets

The All-W Team

MGR	Earl Weaver
COA	Jimmy Williams
SP	Bill Wight
RP	Eddie Watt
C	Earl Williams
1B	Eddie Waitkus
2B	Dick Williams
SS	Ron Washington
3B	Craig Worthington
OF	Gene Woodling
OF	Vic Wertz
OF	Pete Ward
DH	Alan Wiggins

18 • ALL-TIME ROSTER & INDEX

Managers (13)

NAME	YEARS	PAGE
Altobelli, Joe	1983-85	138, 186, 191
Bauer, Hank	1964-68	78, 119, 121, 138, 178, 186, 191
Dykes, Jimmy	1954	140, 191
Harris, Luman	1961	191
Hitchcock, Billy	1962-63	187, 191
Johnson, Davey	1996-97	2-4, 8, 24, 33, 35, 39, 43, 61-63, 71, 75, 77, 79, 82, 90-91, 103, 107, 137, 138, 179, 187, 191, 199
Miller, Ray	1998-	32, 117, 140, 191-192
Oates, Johnny	1991-94	20-21, 25, 134, 137, 138, 191-192, 202
Regan, Phil	1995	53, 191
Richards, Paul	1955-61	78, 123, 138, 140, 189, 191
Ripken, Cal Sr.	1987-88	25, 29, 78, 117, 125, 140, 189, 191-192
Robinson, Frank	1988-91	2, 6, 8, 32, 35, 40, 43, 45-47, 61, 64-65, 69, 71-78, 81, 84, 94-95, 119, 133, 137-139, 147, 164, 167, 174, 182, 189, 191-192, 203
Weaver, Earl	1968-82, 1985-86	10, 25, 29, 32, 77-78, 101, 138, 140, 189, 191-192

Coaches (57)

NAME	YEARS	PAGE
Adair, Jimmy	1957-61	191
Appling, Luke	1963	186, 191
Bamberger, George	1968-77	29, 32, 78, 118, 137, 191, 193
Bauer, Hank	1963	78, 119, 121, 138, 178, 186, 191
Bernhardt, Carlos	1998	140, 191
Biagini, Greg	1992-94	140, 191
Boros, Steve	1995	191
Bosman, Dick	1992-94	28, 32, 191
Brecheen, Harry	1954-67	12, 14, 29, 32, 186, 191
Buford, Don	1988, 1994	31, 41, 62, 78, 81, 88, 100, 103, 107, 120, 125, 129, 135, 139, 157, 177, 186, 191, 194
Bumbry, Al	1995	14, 29, 34, 62, 69, 74, 76, 78, 89, 106, 116, 119-120, 128, 134, 139, 155-156, 166, 186, 191, 194
Busby, Jim	1961	15, 36, 123, 144, 169, 177, 191, 194
Cottier, Chuck	1995	191
Crowley, Terry	1985-88	9, 14, 37, 46, 116, 118, 139, 143, 156, 166, 191, 195
Dobson, Pat	1996	32, 40, 51-52, 63, 139, 166, 186, 191, 196
Down, Rick	1996-98	17, 18, 140, 191
Ermer, Cal	1962	19, 21, 117, 191
Etchebarren, Andy	1996-97	12, 22, 29, 31, 39, 43, 63, 105, 111, 132, 186, 191, 196
Ferraro, Mike	1993	191
Flanagan, Mike	1995, 1998	31, 24, 50-51, 54, 57-59, 63, 65, 69, 72, 76, 78, 97, 114, 116, 130, 134, 139, 143, 187, 191, 196
Frey, Jim	1970-79	15, 21, 29, 140, 191
Harris, Luman	1955-61	191
Hart, John	1988	140, 191
Hendricks, Elrod	1978-	8, 29, 33, 54, 73, 81, 89, 116, 118, 134, 139, 142, 144, 147, 191, 198

NAME	YEARS	PAGE
Hoscheit, Vern	1968	140, 192
Hunter, Billy	1964-77	6, 10, 19, 29, 78, 116, 137-139, 146, 187, 192, 198
Jackson, Al	1989-91	32, 187, 192
Johnson, Darrell	1962	2, 24, 34, 137-138, 146, 163, 187, 192, 199
Lau, Charlie	1969	22, 87, 123, 144, 189, 192, 199
Lollar, Sherman	1964-67	192
Lopes, Davey	1992-94	192
May, Lee	1995	22, 40, 45, 74, 77, 79, 81, 112, 126, 167, 172, 188, 192, 200
McCraw, Tom	1989-91	192
Mendoza, Minnie	1988	192
Miller, Ray	1978-85, 1997	32, 117, 140, 191, 192
Motton, Curt	1989-91	7, 129, 144, 155, 188, 192, 201
Murray, Eddie	1998-	25, 29, 32, 37, 39-41, 43-45, 47, 61-63, 65, 66, 69, 71, 74-76, 81, 84, 87, 94-95, 99-101, 106-108, 111, 119, 126, 130, 133, 135, 139, 144, 147, 157, 188, 192, 201
Narron, Jerry	1993-94	192
Oates, Johnny	1989-91	20-21, 25, 134, 137-139, 191, 192, 202
Oliver, Tom	1954	18, 140, 192
Perlozzo, Sam	1996-	192
Ripken, Cal Sr.	1976-86, 1989-92	25, 29, 78, 117, 125, 140, 189, 191, 192
Robinson, Brooks	1977	2, 6, 8, 29, 31-32, 34-36, 40, 43, 46-47, 61-62, 65, 69, 71-78, 81-84, 86, 90-92, 94, 96, 98, 100-101, 106, 130-132, 140, 189, 192, 203
Robinson, Eddie	1957-59	2, 8, 118, 169, 181, 189, 192, 203
Robinson, Frank	1978-80, 1985-87	2, 8, 32, 35, 40, 43, 45-47, 61, 64-65, 69, 71-78, 81, 84, 94-95, 119, 133, 137-139, 147, 164, 167, 174, 182, 189, 191, 192, 203
Rowe, Ken	1985-86	28, 32, 192, 204
Rowe, Ralph	1981-84	140, 192
Scarborough, Ray	1968	178, 192
Skaff, Frank	1954	192
Staller, George	1962, 1968-75	19, 21, 192
Starrette, Herm	1988	32, 192, 205
Stearns, John	1996-97	192
Vincent, Al	1955-59	140, 192
Weaver, Earl	1968	10, 25, 29, 32, 77-78, 101, 138, 140, 189, 191, 192
Wiley, Mark	1987	32, 192
Williams, Jimmy	1981-87	140, 189, 192
Woodling, Gene	1964-67	36, 62, 74, 78, 107, 139, 145-146, 151, 173, 178, 189, 192, 206

Players (633)

NAME	YEARS	POS	PAGE
Aase, Don	1985-88	RHP	19, 54, 62, 74, 171, 172, 186, 192
Abrams, Cal	1954-55	OF	120, 186, 192
Adair, Jerry	1958-66	2B	6, 30, 40, 82-83, 106, 108, 186, 192
Adams, Bobby	1956	IF	21, 24, 27, 126, 164, 168, 192
Adamson, Mike	1967-69	RHP	28, 58-59, 132, 149, 192
Aldrich, Jay	1990	RHP	192
Alexander, Bob	1955	RHP	105, 192
Alexander, Doyle	1972-76	RHP	11, 30, 34, 40, 147, 176, 186, 192

NAME	YEARS	POS	PAGE
Alexander, Manny	1992-93, 1995-96	2B-SS	*54, 118, 193*
Alomar, Roberto	1996-98	2B	*16, 39, 61, 64-66, 75, 91, 98, 126, 135, 186, 193*
Anderson, Brady	1988-	OF	*19, 21, 29, 39-40, 42-45, 61-62, 65, 84, 91-93, 95, 117, 186, 193*
Anderson, John	1960	RHP	*193*
Anderson, Mike	1978	OF	*126, 149, 174, 186, 193*
Aparicio, Luis	1963-67	SS	*13, 37, 62-65, 75, 77-79, 82-84, 164-165, 176-177, 182, 186, 193*
Arnold, Tony	1986-87	RHP	*193*
Avila, Bobby	1959	2B	*79, 107, 181, 193*
Ayala, Benny	1979-84	OF	*17, 41, 46, 186, 193*
Bailor, Bob	1975-76	IF	*9, 151, 193*
Baines, Harold	1993-95, 1997-	DH	*46, 65-66, 94, 117, 143, 150-151, 165, 177, 186, 193*
Baker, Frank	1973-74	IF	*10, 127, 172, 193*
Ballard, Jeff	1987-91	LHP	*7, 17, 118, 193*
Bamberger, George	1959	RHP	*29, 32, 78, 118, 137, 191, 193*
Barber, Steve	1960-67	LHP	*10, 18, 31, 47, 50-51, 54, 63, 78, 92, 105, 117, 186, 193*
Barberie, Bret	1995	2B	*165, 193*
Barker, Buddy	1960	1B	*193*
Barnowski, Ed	1965-66	RHP	*132, 193*
Bass, Kevin	1995	OF	*9, 28, 164-165, 193*
Bautista, Jose	1988-91	RHP	*193*
Baylor, Don	1970-75	OF	*9, 34, 39, 42, 46, 77, 87, 107, 137, 139, 157, 161, 163, 171-172, 182, 186, 193*
Beamon, Charlie	1956-58	RHP	*25, 36, 53, 119, 126, 193*
Becker, Rich	1998	OF	*193*
Beene, Fred	1968-70	RHP	*15, 59, 106, 193*
Belanger, Mark	1965-81	SS	*13, 29, 34-35, 62, 75, 77-78, 82, 87, 91, 106, 116, 119, 166, 186, 193*
Bell, Eric	1985-87	LHP	*50, 193*
Bell, Juan	1989-91	SS	*11, 109, 118, 126, 147, 193*
Beniquez, Juan	1986	OF	*100, 175, 193*
Benitez, Armando	1994-98	RHP	*16, 186, 193*
Bennett, Joel	1998	RHP	*193*
Berroa, Geronimo	1997	DH/OF	*16, 193*
Berry, Neil	1954	OF	*8, 20, 166, 193*
Bertaina, Frank	1964-67, 1969	LHP	*14, 143, 193*
Besana, Fred	1956	LHP	*36, 193*
Bickford, Vern	1954	RHP	*5, 36, 90, 193*
Birrer, Babe	1956	RHP	*48, 193*
Blair, Paul	1964-76	OF	*5, 14, 29, 39, 42-43, 62, 74-75, 77-78, 106, 116, 166, 186, 193*
Blefary, Curt	1965-68	OF	*39-40, 69, 76, 171, 179, 193*
Blyzka, Mike	1954	RHP	*146, 193*
Boddicker, Mike	1980-88	RHP	*50-51, 54, 56-57, 59, 63, 70-72, 76, 193*
Bolton, Tom	1994	LHP	*175, 193*

NAME	YEARS	POS	PAGE
Bonilla, Bobby	1995-96	3B/OF	*9, 66, 91, 130, 135, 165, 186, 194*
Bonilla, Juan	1986	2B	*194*
Bonner, Bob	1980-83	IF	*101, 155, 194*
Boone, Dan	1990	LHP	*23, 31, 125, 129-130, 194*
Bordi, Rich	1986	RHP	*11, 129, 194*
Bordick, Mike	1997-	SS	*84, 194*
Borowski, Joe	1995	RHP	*27, 194*
Boskie, Shawn	1997	RHP	*114, 194*
Boswell, Dave	1971	RHP	*117, 121, 194*
Bowens, Sam	1963-67	OF	*39, 43, 107, 194*
Bowers, Brent	1996	OF	*105, 194*
Boyd, Bob	1956-60	1B	*5, 9, 146, 186, 194*
Brabender, Gene	1966-68	RHP	*48, 122-123, 133, 194*
Bradley, Phil	1989-90	OF	*14, 21, 46, 87-88, 95, 192, 120, 147, 164, 194*
Brandt, Jackie	1960-65	OF	*14, 20, 46-47, 63, 65, 90*
Breeding, Marv	1960-62	2B	*194*
Brideweser, Jim	1954-57	IF	*5, 143, 164, 178, 194*
Briles, Nellie	1977-78	RHP	*7-8, 14, 109, 118, 171-172, 194*
Brown, Dick	1963-65	C	*2, 11, 17-18, 33, 90, 123, 125, 181, 186, 194*
Brown, Hal	1955-62	RHP	*2, 6, 11, 13, 17-18, 34, 55-56, 58, 78, 194*
Brown, Jarvis	1995	OF	*2, 11, 17-18, 129, 194*
Brown, Kevin	1995	RHP	*2, 6, 11-12, 17-18, 149-150, 174, 194*
Brown, Larry	1973	IF	*2, 8, 11, 17-18, 34, 125, 179, 181, 194*
Brown, Mark	1984	RHP	*2, 11, 17-18, 34, 59, 194*
Brown, Marty	1990	IF	*2, 11, 17-18, 34, 194*
Brunet, George	1963	LHP	*7, 123, 168, 194*
Buford, Damon	1993-95	OF	*113, 117, 125, 194*
Buford, Don	1968-72	OF	*31, 41, 62, 78, 81, 88, 100, 103, 107, 120, 125, 129, 135, 139, 157, 177, 186, 191, 194*
Bumbry, Al	1972-84	OF	*14, 29, 34, 62, 69, 74, 76, 78, 88, 106, 116, 119-120, 128, 134, 139, 155, 156, 166, 186, 191, 194*
Bunker, Wally	1963-68	RHP	*55, 71-72, 92, 132, 151, 194*
Burke, Leo	1958-59	IF/OF	*16, 28, 117, 121, 151, 194*
Burleson, Rick	1987	2B	*14, 28, 109, 175-176, 194*
Burnside, Pete	1963	LHP	*103, 120, 194*
Busby, Jim	1957-58, 1960-61	OF	*15, 36, 123, 144, 169, 177, 191, 194*
Buzhardt, John	1967	RHP	*173, 194*
Byrd, Harry	1956	RHP	*9, 17-18, 122, 144, 194*
Cabell, Enos	1972-74	1B	*157, 186, 194*
Carey, Paul	1993	1B	*17, 194*
Carrasquel, Chico	1959	SS	*9, 12, 15-16, 28, 79, 177, 186, 194*
Carreon, Camilo	1966	C	*15-16, 122-123, 126, 177, 194*
Carter, Joe	1998	DH	*24, 65-66, 94, 181, 186, 194*
Castleman, Foster	1958	IF	*180, 194*
Causey, Wayne	1955-57	IF	*131-132, 146, 186, 194*
Ceccarelli, Art	1957	LHP	*59, 112, 194*
Chakales, Bob	1954	RHP	*164, 194*
Charlton, Norm	1998	LHP	*65, 167, 194*
Chevez, Tony	1977	RHP	*108, 194*

NAME	YEARS	POS	PAGE
Chism, Tom	1979	1B	*195*
Cimoli, Gino	1964	OF	*14, 195*
Clark, Terry	1995	RHP	*21, 186, 195*
Clements, Pat	1992	LHP	*112, 195*
Clyburn, Danny	1997-98	OF	*195*
Coan, Gil	1954-55	OF	*6, 15, 36, 169, 186, 195*
Coggins, Rich	1972-74	OF	*21, 129, 186, 195*
Coleman, Joe	1954-55	RHP	*26, 34, 48, 122-123, 126, 195*
Coleman, Rip	1959-60	LHP	*34, 112, 195*
Connally, Fritz	1985	3B	*195*
Consuegra, Sandy	1956-57	RHP	*36, 79, 176, 195*
Cook, Mike	1993	RHP	*10, 21, 195*
Coppinger, Rocky	1996-	RHP	*7, 12, 71, 130, 195*
Corbin, Archie	1996	RHP	*195*
Corbett, Doug	1987	RHP	*195*
Corey, Mark	1979-81	OF	*12, 157, 195*
Courtney, Clint	1954, 1960, 1961	C	*9, 33, 74, 90, 123, 129, 133, 142, 146, 164, 169, 174, 186, 195*
Cox, Billy	1955	3B	*22-23, 131, 195*
Criscione, Dave	1977	C	*129, 195*
Crowley, Terry	1969-73, 1976-82	1B/OF/DH	*9, 14, 37, 46, 116, 118, 139, 143, 156, 186, 191, 195*
Cruz, Todd	1983-84	3B	*15, 54, 98, 186, 195*
Cuellar, Mike	1969-76	LHP	*47-48, 51, 53, 55-59, 62-63, 69-70, 74, 76, 78-79, 96-97, 166, 186, 195*
Dagres, Angie	1955	OF	*8, 19, 21, 27-29, 33, 36, 121, 195*
Dalrymple, Clay	1969-71	C	*120, 172, 195*
Dauer, Rich	1976-85	2B	*37, 67, 82, 101, 105-106, 111, 134, 148, 155-156, 186, 195*
DaVanon, Jerry	1971	IF	*186, 195*
Davis, Eric	1997-98	OF	*2, 65, 73-74, 94, 114, 167, 186, 195*
Davis, Glenn	1991-93	1B	*2, 8, 34, 147-148, 150, 186, 195*
Davis, Storm	1982-86, 1992	RHP	*2, 8, 12, 19, 112, 143, 195*
Davis, Tommy	1972-75	DH	*2, 6, 103, 145, 164, 171, 173, 186, 195*
Davis, Butch	1988-89	OF	*2, 195*
DeCinces, Doug	1973-81	3B	*9, 37, 43-45, 66, 77, 100-102, 107, 111, 134, 163, 186, 195*
Dedrick, Jim	1995	RHP	*59, 195*
de la Rosa, Francisco	1991	RHP	*16, 19, 59, 195*
DeLeon, Luis	1987	RHP	*195*
Dellucci, David	1997	OF	*4, 19, 151, 195*
Delock, Ike	1963	RHP	*15, 163, 175, 195*
Dempsey, Rick	1976-86, 1992	C	*6, 21, 29, 43, 74, 76, 79, 81, 89, 98, 106, 125, 130, 134, 142, 145, 147, 186, 195*
DeSilva, John	1995	RHP	*195*
Devereaux, Mike	1989-94, 1996	OF	*42, 46, 74-75, 114, 142, 186, 195*
Devarez, Cesar	1995-96	C	*37, 195*
Diering, Chuck	1954-56	OF	*15, 74, 113, 171, 180, 186, 195*
Dillard, Gordon	1988	LHP	*147, 195*

NAME	YEARS	POS	PAGE
Dillman, Bill	1967	RHP	*196*
Dimmel, Mike	1977-78	OF	*196*
Dixon, Ken	1984-87	RHP	*59, 116, 196*
Dobson, Pat	1971-72	RHP	*32, 40, 54-52, 64, 139, 166, 186, 191, 196*
Dodd, Tom	1986	3B	*196*
Dorish, Harry	1955-56	RHP	*164, 196*
Drabek, Doug	1998	RHP	*65, 76, 182, 196*
Drabowsky, Moe	1966-68, 1970	RHP	*52, 118, 143, 151, 173, 186, 196*
Drago, Dick	1977	RHP	*196*
Dropo, Walt	1959-61	1B	*13, 16, 28, 109, 175, 182, 196*
Dukes, Tom	1971	RHP	*15, 18, 21, 196*
Duncan, Dave	1975-76	C	*15, 87, 90, 170, 179, 196*
Duren, Ryne	1954	RHP	*32, 65, 90, 105, 133, 176, 196*
Durham, Joe	1954, 1957	OF	*36, 105, 112, 116, 121, 196*
Dwyer, Jim	1981-88	OF/DH	*45, 100, 171, 196*
Dyck, Jim	1955-56	OF	*36, 196*
Dykhoff, Radhames	1998	LHP	*108, 125, 196*
Eichhorn, Mark	1993-94	RHP	*196*
Epstein, Mike	1966-67	1B	*33, 130, 155-157, 168, 171, 179, 196*
Erickson, Scott	1995-	RHP	*7, 14, 42, 52, 54, 58, 96, 111, 196*
Essegian, Chuck	1961	OF/PH	*9, 21, 90, 120, 196*
Estrada, Chuck	1960-64	RHP	*19, 21, 41, 48, 56-58, 63, 71-73, 105, 196*
Etchebarren, Andy	1962, 1965-75	C	*12, 22, 29, 32, 39, 46, 66,*
			105, 111, 132, 186, 191, 196
Evans, Dwight	1991	OF	*46, 94, 109, 175, 196*
Evers, Hoot	1955-56	OF	*12, 28, 94, 109, 123, 143, 166, 196*
Farmer, Ed	1977	RHP	*10, 21, 28, 90, 176, 181, 196*
Fernandez, Chico	1968	IF	*16, 121, 196*
Fernandez, Sid	1994-95	LHP	*6, 25, 40, 179, 196*
Ferrarese, Don	1955-57	LHP	*30, 36, 105, 121, 196*
Finigan, Jim	1959	3B	*122, 133, 187, 196*
Finley, Steve	1989-90	OF	*147-148, 155-156, 163, 187, 196*
Fiore, Mike	1968	1B	*151, 196*
Fisher, Eddie	1966-67	RHP	*8, 56, 176, 196*
Fisher, Jack	1959-62	RHP	*41, 43, 48, 88, 117, 196*
Fisher, Tom	1967	RHP	*8, 105, 112, 196*
Flanagan, Mike	1975-87, 1991-92	LHP	*29, 32, 50-51, 54, 57-58, 63, 65, 69, 72, 76,*
			78, 97, 114, 116, 130, 134, 139, 143, 187, 191, 196
Flinn, John	1978-79, 1982	RHP	*144, 196*
Floyd, Bobby	1968-70	IF	*14, 18, 105, 187, 196*
Foiles, Hank	1961	C	*15, 187, 196*
Forbes, P.J.	1998	2B	*187, 196*
Ford, Dan	1982-85	OF	*10, 14, 24, 39, 46, 111,*
			133, 149, 171-172, 187, 196
Ford, Dave	1978-81	RHP	*10, 24, 148, 196*
Fornieles, Mike	1956-57	RHP	*59, 65, 79, 118, 165, 196*
Fox, Howie	1954	RHP	*7, 22, 121, 167, 196*
Francona, Tito	1956-57	OF/1B	*8, 12, 16, 71, 90, 126, 138, 164, 187, 196*
Frazier, Joe	1956	OF	*21, 137, 196*

NAME	YEARS	POS	PAGE
Freed, Roger	1970	OF	*31, 155, 197*
Fridley, Jim	1954	OF	*30, 122, 146, 163, 181, 187, 197*
Frohwirth, Todd	1991-93	RHP	*187, 197*
Fuller, Jim	1973-74	OF	*18, 117, 155-157, 187, 197*
Fussell, Chris	1998	RHP	*197*
Gaines, Joe	1963-64	OF	*15, 187, 197*
Gallagher, Dave	1990	OF	*4, 197*
Garcia, Chico	1954	2B	*12, 16, 105, 129, 158, 197*
Garcia, Kiko	1976-80	IF	*12, 16, 97, 105, 111, 197*
Gardner, Billy	1956-59	2B	*10, 19, 23, 74, 82, 137, 169, 173, 180, 187, 197*
Garland, Wayne	1973-76	RHP	*6, 11, 19, 21, 28, 51, 197*
Gastall, Tom	1955-56	C	*19, 21, 33, 122-123, 197*
Gentile, Jim	1960-63	1B	*21, 40, 45-46, 61, 63, 65, 71, 76-75, 78, 81, 83, 95, 102, 111, 187, 197*
Gerhart, Ken	1986-88	OF	*42, 89, 101, 105, 156, 187, 197*
Gilliford, Paul	1967	LHP	*14, 105, 197*
Ginsberg, Joe	1956-60	C	*7, 35, 121, 166-167, 187, 197*
Gomez, Leo	1990-95	3B	*16, 21, 133, 187, 197*
Gonzales, Rene	1987-90	IF	*14, 101, 187, 197*
Goodman, Billy	1957	IF	*21, 175, 197*
Goodwin, Curtis	1995	OF	*197*
Graham, Dan	1980-81	C	*11, 20, 157, 197*
Gray, Ted	1955	LHP	*11, 36, 59, 113, 176, 197*
Green, Gene	1960	OF/C	*9, 11, 15, 90, 121, 151, 197*
Green, Lenny	1957-59, 1964	OF	*11, 36, 144, 146, 187, 197*
Greene, Charlie	1997-98	C	*8-9, 19, 197*
Greene, Willie	1998-	OF	*8, 197*
Grich, Bob	1970-76	2B	*4, 34, 39, 44, 61, 75, 77, 79, 85, 91, 99-100, 134, 148, 155-157, 163, 170, 187, 197*
Griffin, Mike	1987	RHP	*59, 187, 197*
Grimsley, Ross	1974-77, 1982	LHP	*26, 116, 126, 144, 187, 197*
Gross, Wayne	1984-85	3B	*42, 197*
Guillen, Ozzie	1998	SS	*31, 65-66, 177, 197*
Gulliver, Glenn	1982-83	3B	*197*
Gutierrez, Jackie	1986-87	IF	*197*
Guzman, Juan	1998-	RHP	*197*
Habyan, John	1985-88	RHP	*15, 197*
Haddix, Harvey	1964-65	LHP	*9, 109, 123, 171, 197*
Hairston, Jerry	1998-	2B	*126, 197*
Hale, Bob	1955-59	1B	*31, 36, 187, 197*
Hall, Dick	1961-66, 1969-71	RHP	*15, 19, 21, 48, 78, 117, 120, 129-130, 144, 187, 197*
Hammonds, Jeffrey	1993-98	OF	*148, 150, 187, 197*
Hamric, Bert	1958	OF/PH	*6, 197*
Haney, Larry	1966-68	C	*6, 126, 151, 179, 197*
Hansen, Ron	1958-62	SS	*8, 40, 46-47, 61, 69, 71, 73, 76, 105, 116,169, 187, 197*
Hardin, Jim	1967-71	RHP	*47, 58, 122-123, 187, 197*
Harlow, Larry	1975-79	OF	*14, 19, 54, 102, 171, 187, 197*

NAME	YEARS	POS	PAGE
Harnisch, Pete	1988-90	RHP	28, 59, 66, 147-148, 198
Harper, Tommy	1976	DH	109, 164, 167, 198
Harris, Gene	1995	RHP	37, 198
Harrison, Bob	1955-56	RHP	24, 36, 198
Harrison, Roric	1972	RHP	24, 28, 156, 198
Harshman, Jack	1958-59	LHP	21, 47-48, 198
Hart, Mike	1987	OF	18, 21, 112, 198
Hartley, Mike	1995	RHP	198
Hartzell, Paul	1980	RHP	198
Hatton, Grady	1956	IF	6, 27, 33, 137, 164, 167, 198
Havens, Brad	1985-86	LHP	198
Haynes, Jimmy	1995-96	RHP	198
Hazewood, Drungo	1980	OF	5, 16, 148, 198
Heard, Jehosie	1954	LHP	105, 129-130, 198
Held, Mel	1956	RHP	198
Held, Woodie	1966-67	IF/OF	198
Hendricks, Elrod	1968-72, 1973-76, 1978-79	C	8, 29, 33, 54, 73, 81, 89, 116, 118, 134, 139, 142, 144, 147, 191, 198
Hernandez, Leo	1982-83, 1985	3B	16, 187, 198
Herzog, Whitey	1961-62	OF	12, 137-138, 146, 164, 187, 198
Hickey, Kevin	1989-91	LHP	113, 177, 198
Hoeft, Billy	1959-62	LHP	48, 163, 176, 198
Hoiles, Chris	1989-	C	30, 39, 43-45, 74, 81, 84, 89, 90, 98, 198
Holdsworth, Fred	1976-77	RHP	113, 198
Holton, Brian	1989-90	RHP	147, 198
Holtzman, Ken	1976	LHP	40, 147, 172, 179, 198
Hood, Don	1973-74	LHP	15, 40, 148, 198
Horn, Sam	1990-92	1B/DH	46, 88, 95, 106, 130, 175, 187, 198
Houtteman, Art	1957	RHP	28, 36, 118, 176, 198
Howard, Bruce	1968	RHP	7, 48, 59, 112, 117, 126, 198
Hudler, Rex	1986	IF	149, 172, 198
Huffman, Phil	1985	RHP	198
Hughes, Keith	1988	OF	173, 198
Huismann, Mark	1989	RHP	198
Hulett, Tim	1989-94	IF	187, 189, 198
Hunter, Billy	1954	SS	6, 10, 19, 29, 78, 116, 137-139, 146, 187, 192, 198
Huppert, Dave	1983	C	198
Huson, Jeff	1995-96	IF	23, 198
Hutto, Jim	1975	C	16, 33, 198
Hyde, Dick	1961	RHP	15, 17, 133, 169, 198
Incaviglia, Pete	1996-97	OF/DH	37, 102, 149, 198
Jackson, Grant	1971-76	LHP	8, 24, 48, 52, 54, 59, 147, 172, 174, 187, 198
Jackson, Lou	1964	OF	24, 103, 187, 198
Jackson, Reggie	1976	OF	8, 24, 42, 45-46, 67, 77, 81, 133, 149, 163, 168, 171-172, 175, 179-180, 182, 187, 198
Jackson, Ron	1984	3B	24, 187, 198
Jefferson, Jesse	1973-75	RHP	24, 198
Jefferson, Stan	1989-90	OF	24, 113, 149, 173, 179, 187, 198

NAME	YEARS	POS	PAGE
Johns, Doug	1998	LHP	*199*
Johnson, Bob	1963-67	IF	*2, 4, 8, 24, 35, 100, 106, 121, 169, 187, 199*
Johnson, Connie	1956-58	RHP	*2, 8, 24, 34, 50, 199*
Johnson, Darrell	1962	C	*2, 24, 34, 13-138, 146, 163, 187, 192, 199*
Johnson, Davey	1965-72	2B	*3, 4, 8, 24, 33, 35, 39, 43, 61-63, 71, 75, 77, 79, 82, 90-91, 103, 107, 137-138, 179, 187, 191, 199*
Johnson, Dave	1989-91	RHP	*2, 3, 5, 24, 117, 187, 199*
Johnson, David	1974-75	RHP	*2, 3, 5, 24, 199*
Johnson, Don	1955	RHP	*2, 24, 199*
Johnson, Ernie	1959	RHP	*2, 24, 199*
Johnson, Mike	1997	RHP	*2, 3, 24, 59, 199*
Jones, Doug	1995	RHP	*2, 164, 199*
Jones, Gordon	1960-61	RHP	*2, 112, 123, 199*
Jones, Odell	1986	RHP	*2, 14, 31, 199*
Jones, Ricky	1986	IF	*2, 37, 187, 199*
Jones, Sam	1964	RHP	*2, 199*
Jones, Stacy	1991	RHP	*2, 15, 129, 199*
Kamieniecki, Scott	1997-	RHP	*22, 172, 199*
Kell, George	1956-57	3B	*61, 77, 82, 94, 109, 126, 158, 188, 199*
Kellert, Frank	1954	1B	*36, 122, 164, 188, 199*
Kelly, Pat	1977-80	OF	*6, 14, 17, 45-46, 116, 127, 177, 188, 199*
Kennedy, Bob	1954-55	3B	*4, 24, 113, 125, 137-139, 177, 199*
Kennedy, Terry	1987-88	C	*24, 61, 66, 88, 125, 149, 188, 199*
Kerrigan, Joe	1978, 1980	RHP	*199*
Key, Jimmy	1997-98	LHP	*18, 21-22, 65-66, 109, 172, 176, 188, 199*
Kilgus, Paul	1991	LHP	*7, 27, 37, 112, 199*
Kingsdale, Eugene	1996, 1998	OF	*108, 199*
Kinnunen, Mike	1986-87	LHP	*199*
Kirkland, Willie	1964	OF	*103, 169, 188, 199*
Kittle, Ron	1990	1B/DH	*66, 133, 147, 177, 182, 188, 199*
Klaus, Billy	1959-60	IF	*11, 23, 45, 126, 151, 163, 169, 172, 188, 199*
Klingenbeck, Scott	1994-95	RHP	*22, 199*
Knight, Ray	1987	3B	*17-18, 21, 34, 88, 137, 167, 179, 181-182, 199*
Knowles, Darold	1965	LHP	*147, 169, 171, 179, 188, 199*
Kokos, Dick	1954	OF	*6, 20, 122, 129, 199*
Komminsk, Brad	1990	OF	*8, 149, 188, 199*
Koslo, Dave	1954	LHP	*6, 122, 180, 199*
Krenchicki, Wayne	1979-81	IF	*188, 199*
Kretlow, Lou	1954-55	RHP	*199*
Krivda, Rick	1995-97	RHP	*27, 199*
Kryhoski, Dick	1954	1B	*146, 172, 199*
Kuzava, Bob	1954-55	LHP	*36, 59, 178, 199*
Lacy, Lee	1985-87	OF	*9, 39, 119, 188, 199*
Laker, Tim	1997	C	*12, 199*
Landrith, Hobie	1962-63	C	*169, 199*
Landrum, Tito	1983, 1988	OF	*12, 16, 142, 171, 188, 199*
Larsen, Don	1954, 1965	RHP	*48, 58, 144, 146, 164, 168, 173-174, 180, 182, 188, 199*
Lau, Charlie	1961-63, 1964-67	C	*22, 87, 123, 144, 189, 192, 199*

NAME	YEARS	POS	PAGE
Ledesma, Aaron	1997	IF	4, 151, 188, 200
Lee, Mark	1995	LHP	7, 14, 17, 22, 114, 200
Lefferts, Craig	1992	LHP	35, 118, 200
Lehew, Jim	1961-62	RHP	113, 117, 200
Lehman, Ken	1957-58	LHP	200
Lenhardt, Don	1954	OF	200
Leonard, Mark	1993	OF	7, 112, 200
Leonhard, Dave	1967-72	RHP	4, 117, 119-120, 156, 188, 200
Leppert, Don	1955	2B	18, 41, 105, 129, 146, 188, 200
Lewis, Richie	1992, 1998	RHP	21, 144, 151, 200
Littlefield, Dick	1954	LHP	20, 22, 173, 200
Locke, Charlie	1955	RHP	21, 31, 200
Lockman, Whitey	1959	1B	12, 34, 41, 137, 139, 180, 188, 200
Loes, Billy	1956-59	RHP	62, 200
Lopat, Eddie	1955	LHP	6, 33, 109, 137-138, 176-178, 200
Lopez, Carlos	1978	OF	188, 200
Lopez, Marcelino	1967, 1969-70	LHP	118, 200
Lowenstein, John	1979-85	OF	22, 45-46, 77, 83, 96, 100, 120, 133-134, 181, 188, 200
Luebber, Steve	1981	RHP	200
Luebke, Dick	1962	LHP	200
Lynn, Fred	1985-88	OF	34, 40, 42, 47, 66, 94, 166, 175, 182, 188, 200
Mabe, Bobbie	1960	RHP	200
Maddox, Elliott	1977	OF	166, 173, 200
Majeski, Hank	1955	3B	27, 36, 109, 122, 200
Manto, Jeff	1995	3B	39-40, 155-157, 181, 188, 200
Marquis, Roger	1955	OF	89-90, 131-132, 200
Marsh, Fred	1955-56	IF	200
Marshall, Jim	1958	1B	10, 21, 103, 105, 137-139, 200
Martin, Morrie	1956	LHP	21, 173, 200
Martinez, Chito	1991-93	OF	12, 16, 108, 200
Martinez, Dennis	1976-86	RHP	6, 8, 26, 29, 37, 55, 57-58, 66, 70, 108, 134, 146, 163, 200
Martinez, Tippy	1976-86	LHP	8, 12, 29, 34, 63, 66, 116, 144, 147, 166, 172, 200
Matchick, Tom	1972	3B	166, 200
Mathews, Terry	1996-98	RHP	200
Maxwell, Charlie	1955	OF	36, 200
May, Dave	1967-70	OF	4, 22, 46, 126, 188, 200
May, Lee	1975-80	1B/DH	22, 40, 45, 74, 77, 79, 81, 112, 126, 167, 172, 188, 192, 200
May, Rudy	1976-77	LHP	8, 22, 133, 145, 147, 200
McCormick, Mike	1963-64	LHP	21, 48, 59, 65, 173, 182, 200
McDonald, Ben	1989-95	RHP	6, 13, 19, 21, 53, 105, 129, 148, 150, 200
McDonald, Jim	1955	RHP	21, 36, 146, 178, 200
McDowell, Roger	1996	RHP	59, 112, 179, 200
McGehee, Kevin	1993	RHP	200
McGregor, Scott	1976-88	LHP	29, 51, 55-56, 58-59, 63, 78, 101, 111, 116, 119, 135, 145, 147, 149, 200

NAME	YEARS	POS	PAGE
McGuire, Mickey	1962, 1967	IF	*103, 201*
McKnight, Jeff	1990-91	IF/OF	*23, 126, 133, 201*
McLemore, Mark	1992-94	2B/OF	*9, 188, 201*
McNally, Dave	1962-74	LHP	*4, 18, 29, 43-44, 46-48, 50-53, 55, 57, 62-63, 70-71, 74, 77-78, 104, 108, 118, 132, 166, 188, 201*
Mele, Sam	1954	OF	*33, 36, 137, 164, 169, 201*
Melendez, Francisco	1989	1B	*16, 174, 201*
Melvin, Bob	1989-91	C	*4, 14, 89, 150, 188, 201*
Mercedes, Luis	1991-93	OF	*10, 19, 21, 35, 155, 201*
Mercker, Kent	1996	LHP	*149, 201*
Mesa, Jose	1987, 1990-92	RHP	*163, 172, 201*
Miksis, Eddie	1957-58	IF	*201*
Milacki, Bob	1988-92	RHP	*4, 50, 201*
Milchin, Mike	1996	LHP	*201*
Miller, Bill	1955	LHP	*2-3, 31, 146, 164, 178, 201*
Miller, Dyar	1975-77	RHP	*2, 34, 201*
Miller, John	1962-63, 1965-67	RHP	*2-3, 11, 28, 34, 113, 117, 201*
Miller, Randy	1977	RHP	*2, 8, 34, 90, 201*
Miller, Stu	1963-67	RHP	*2, 7-8, 10, 34, 43, 50, 56, 58, 65, 74, 78, 92, 120, 165, 188, 201*
Milligan, Randy	1989-92	1B	*13, 39, 87, 107, 130, 201*
Mills, Alan	1992-98	RHP	*20, 27, 59, 135, 201*
Minor, Ryan	1998-	3B	*201*
Mirabella, Paul	1983	LHP	*201*
Miranda, Willy	1955-59	SS	*18, 79, 90-91, 116, 123, 130, 135, 146, 178, 188, 201*
Mitchell, John	1990	RHP	*126, 179, 201*
Mitchell, Paul	1975	RHP	*201*
Moeller, Ron	1956, 1958	LHP	*131-132, 151, 201*
Molinaro, Bob	1979	OF	*173, 201*
Moore, Ray	1955-57	RHP	*15, 47, 117, 123, 201*
Mora, Andres	1976-78	OF	*188, 201*
Morales, Jose	1981-82	C/PH	*79, 118, 201*
Moreland, Keith	1989	DH	*18, 109, 201*
Morgan, Mike	1988	RHP	*59, 66, 103, 149, 201*
Morogiello, Dan	1983	LHP	*201*
Morris, John	1968	LHP	*151, 201*
Moss, Les	1954-55	C	*33, 90, 137, 201*
Motton, Curt	1967-71, 1973-74	OF	*7, 129, 144, 155, 188, 192, 201*
Mouton, Lyle	1998	OF	*37, 102, 201*
Moyer, Jamie	1993-95	LHP	*201*
Munoz, Bobby	1998	RHP	*37, 201*
Murray, Eddie	1977-88, 1996	1B	*25, 29, 32, 37, 39-41, 43-45, 47, 61-63, 65, 66, 69, 71, 74-76, 81, 84, 87, 94-95, 99-101, 106-108, 111, 119, 126, 130, 133, 135, 139, 144, 147, 157, 188, 192, 201*
Murray, Ray	1954	C	*28, 201*
Muser, Tony	1975-77	1B	*102, 137, 139, 201*
Mussina, Mike	1991-	RHP	*9, 12, 21, 50, 54-57, 59, 62-63, 65, 70, 75, 148, 150, 156, 201*

NAME	YEARS	POS	PAGE
Myers, Jimmy	1996	RHP	8, 202
Myers, Randy	1996-97	LHP	8, 5-6, 62, 70-71, 74, 178, 202
Narum, Buster	1963	RHP	5, 41, 48, 202
Nelson, Bob	1955-57	OF	4, 7, 14, 101, 132, 202
Nelson, Roger	1968	RHP	14, 133, 151, 202
Nichols, Carl	1986-88	C	21, 105, 202
Nicholson, Dave	1960, 1962	OF	4, 112, 202
Niedenfuer, Tom	1987-88	RHP	7, 202
Nieman, Bob	1956-59	OF	4, 21, 41, 74, 102, 123, 202
Nixon, Donell	1990	OF	24, 37, 126, 202
Nokes, Matt	1995	C	112, 202
Nolan, Joe	1982-85	C	7, 28, 133, 202
Noles, Dickie	1988	RHP	202
Nordbrook, Tim	1974-76	SS	35, 113, 117, 202
Northrup, Jim	1974-75	OF	21, 109, 166, 202
Oates, Johnny	1970, 1972	C	20-21, 25, 134, 137, 138, 191-193, 202
Obando, Sherman	1993, 1995	OF	202
O'Connor, Jack	1987	LHP	202
O'Dell, Billy	1954, 1956-59	LHP	14, 31, 34, 36, 47, 59, 61-62, 76, 105, 202
O'Donoghue, John P.	1993	LHP	125, 129, 202
O'Donoghue, John E.	1968	LHP	113, 116, 121, 125, 202
Oertel, Chuck	1958	OF	129, 202
Oliver, Bob	1974	OF/1B	4, 18, 126, 202
Olson, Gregg	1988-93	RHP	14, 25, 50, 63, 69, 74, 76, 148, 202
O'Malley, Tom	1985-86	3B	28, 103, 202
Oquist, Mike	1993-95	RHP	59, 202
Orosco, Jesse	1995-	LHP	56, 65-66, 111, 130, 179, 181, 202
Orsino, John	1963-65	C	7, 14, 89, 202
Orsulak, Joe	1988-92	OF	15, 46, 202
Otanez, Willis	1998	OF	202
Pacella, John	1984	RHP	202
Pagan, Dave	1976	RHP	21, 145, 147, 150, 202
Pagliarulo, Mike	1993	3B	31, 37, 172, 188, 202
Palica, Erv	1955-56	RHP	6, 202
Palmer, Jim	1965-67, 1969-84	RHP	29, 32, 35, 37, 47, 50-51, 54-57, 61-63, 67 69-78, 92, 97, 100-101, 106, 116, 134, 188, 202
Palmeiro, Rafael	1994-98	1B	45, 62, 65-66, 74-75, 91, 96-97, 134, 149-150, 188, 202
Papa, John	1961-62	RHP	6, 21, 202
Pappas, Milt	1957-65	RHP	6, 36, 41, 47-48, 50, 58, 61-62, 77-78, 131, 147, 202
Pardo, Al	1985-86	C	118, 202
Parent, Mark	1992-93, 1996	C	21, 31, 37, 145, 188, 202
Paris, Kelly	1985-86	IF	15, 37, 133, 171, 188, 202
Parrott, Mike	1977	RHP	9, 133, 148, 156, 202
Patton, Tom	1957	C	21, 33, 89, 90, 202
Pearson, Albie	1959-60	OF	45, 129-130, 146, 151, 182, 202
Pena, Orlando	1971, 1973	RHP	16, 130, 202
Pennington, Brad	1993-95	LHP	14, 37, 129, 202

NAME	YEARS	POS	PAGE
Peraza, Oswald	1988	RHP	203
Peterson, Buddy	1957	IF	103, 133, 188, 203
Philley, Dave	1955-56, 1960-61	OF/1B	4, 12, 33, 37, 74, 107, 118, 130, 145, 174, 177, 188, 203
Phoebus, Tom	1966-70	RHP	47, 50, 53, 72, 92, 113, 117, 121, 129, 203
Pickering, Calvin	1998-	1B	20, 118, 157, 203
Pilarcik, Al	1957-60	OF	34, 90-91, 107, 120, 146, 188, 203
Pillette, Duane	1954-55	RHP	126, 203
Piniella, Lou	1964	OF	137, 163, 182, 202
Polonia, Luis	1996	OF	129-130, 188, 203
Ponson, Sidney	1998	RHP	108, 125, 203
Poole, Jim	1991-94	LHP	15, 188, 203
Pope, Dave	1955-56	OF	10, 21, 203
Portocarrero, Arnie	1958-60	RHP	22, 28, 48, 203
Powell, Boog	1961-74	1B	12, 29, 39-40, 42-43, 47, 61-63, 69, 71, 73-74, 76-78, 81, 87, 99, 106, 126, 130, 132, 156, 166, 188, 203
Powers, John	1960	OF	107, 203
Powis, Carl	1957	OF	107, 203
Price, Joe	1990	LHP	203
Pyburn, Jim	1955-57	OF	101, 203
Quirk, Art	1962	LHP	114, 203
Quirk, Jamie	1989	C	149, 203
Ramirez, Allan	1983	RHP	203
Rayford, Floyd	1980, 1982, 1984-87	3B/C	13-14, 43, 145, 189, 203
Reboulet, Jeff	1997-	IF	23, 203
Reinbach, Mike	1974	OF	12, 103, 157, 203
Rettenmund, Merv	1968-73	OF	120, 155-157, 171, 189, 203
Reynolds, Bob	1972-75	RHP	4, 12, 102, 149, 203
Reynolds, Harold	1993	2B	19, 37, 126, 164, 203
Rhodes, Arthur	1991-	LHP	7, 203
Rice, Del	1960	C	6, 20, 90, 123, 137, 171, 203
Richert, Pete	1967-71	LHP	119, 167, 189, 203
Rineer, Jeff	1979	LHP	89-90, 203
Ripken, Bill	1987-92, 1996	2B	8, 22, 34, 42, 82, 100, 112, 117, 125, 145, 189, 203
Ripken, Cal Jr.	1981-	SS	8, 29, 34-35, 39-40, 42, 46-47, 61-62, 64-66, 69, 71-76, 81-83, 84, 87, 91, 93-95, 98, 100, 106, 112, 117, 125, 155, 189, 203
Roberts, Robin	1962-65	RHP	9, 19, 56, 59, 77, 135, 165, 174, 189, 203
Robinson, Brooks	1955-77	3B	2, 5, 6, 8, 29, 31-32, 34-36, 40, 43, 46-47, 61-62, 65, 69, 71-78, 81-84, 86, 90-92, 94, 96, 98, 100-101, 106, 130-132, 140, 189, 192, 203
Robinson, Earl	1961-62, 1964	OF	5, 8, 34, 107, 189, 203
Robinson, Eddie	1957	1B	5, 8, 118, 169, 181, 189, 192, 203
Robinson, Frank	1966-71	OF	2, 5, 8, 32, 35, 40, 43, 45-47, 61, 64-65, 69, 71-78, 81, 84, 94-95, 119, 133, 137-139, 147, 164, 167, 174, 182, 189, 191, 192, 203
Robinson, Jeff	1991	RHP	5, 34, 129-130, 203
Robles, Sergio	1972-73	C	16, 33, 203
Rodriguez, Aurelio	1983	3B	16, 79, 168, 203
Rodriguez, Nerio	1996-98	RHP	16, 27, 105, 203
Rodriguez, Vic	1984	2B	189, 203

204 *The Book of Baltimore Orioles Lists*

NAME	YEARS	POS	PAGE
Roenicke, Gary	1978-85	OF	12, 40, 43, 83, 91, 100, 106, 111, 126, 134, 149, 204
Rosario, Melvin	1997	C	14, 204
Rogovin, Saul	1955	RHP	204
Rowdon, Wade	1988	3B	103, 167, 204
Rowe, Ken	1964-65	RHP	28, 32, 192, 204
Royster, Willie	1981	C	15, 204
Roznovsky, Vic	1966-67	C	42-43, 204
Rudolph, Ken	1977	C	11, 204
Sabo, Chris	1994	3B/OF	28, 66, 133, 167, 182, 204
Sackinsky, Brian	1996	RHP	204
Sakata, Lenn	1980-85	IF	12, 47, 133, 189, 204
Salmon, Chico	1969-72	IF	9, 12, 16, 100-101, 204
Sanchez, Orlando	1984	C	16, 204
Saverine, Bob	1959, 1962-64	IF/OF	4, 131-132, 169, 204
Scarsone, Steve	1992-93	IF	174, 204
Schallock, Art	1955	LHP	36, 178, 204
Scherrer, Bill	1988	LHP	133, 204
Schilling, Curt	1988-90	RHP	21, 114, 147-148, 204
Schmidt, Dave	1987-89	RHP	50, 204
Schmitz, Johnny	1956	LHP	6, 12, 178, 204
Schneider, Jeff	1981	LHP	59, 204
Schu, Rick	1988-89	3B	17, 31, 113, 174, 204
Scott, Mickey	1972-73	LHP	7, 14, 118, 204
Segrist, Kal	1955	IF	146, 178, 204
Segui, David	1990-93	1B/OF	4, 37, 127, 204
Severinsen, Al	1969	RHP	204
Sheets, Larry	1984-89	OF/DH	7, 15, 42, 45, 74, 100, 102, 134, 189, 204
Shelby, John	1981-87	OF	22, 43, 108, 135, 204
Shepherd, Keith	1996	RHP	10, 204
Shetrone, Barry	1959-62	OF	113, 117, 204
Shields, Tommy	1992	IF	112, 204
Shopay, Tom	1971-72, 1975-77	OF	172, 204
Short, Billy	1962, 1966	LHP	173, 204
Siebern, Norm	1964-65	1B	62, 147, 157, 172, 188, 204
Simmons, Nelson	1987	OF	14, 158, 166, 204
Singleton, Ken	1975-84	OF/DH	29, 34, 46, 61-62, 64, 70, 72, 74-75, 78, 82, 104, 113, 116, 127, 135, 188, 204
Sisk, Doug	1988	RHP	179, 204
Skaggs, Dave	1977-80	C	4, 7, 188, 204
Sleater, Lou	1958	LHP	5, 113, 117, 204
Smith, Al	1963	OF	2, 107, 121, 177, 183, 204
Smith, Billy	1977-79	2B	2, 23, 189, 204
Smith, Dwight	1994	OF	2, 8, 204
Smith, Hal	1955-56	C	2, 103, 146, 204
Smith, Lee	1994	RHP	2, 7-8, 14, 18, 56, 62, 64, 66, 70, 129, 204
Smith, Lonnie	1993-94	OF	2, 8, 34, 149, 174, 204
Smith, Mark	1994-96	OF	2, 8, 34, 39-40, 148, 150, 204
Smith, Mike	1989-90	RHP	2-4, 112, 204

NAME	YEARS	POS	PAGE
Smith, Nate	1962	C	2, 8, 34, 205
Smith, Pete	1998	RHP	2, 205
Smith, Roy	1991	RHP	2, 34, 183, 205
Snell, Nate	1984-86	RHP	205
Snyder, Russ	1961-67	OF	107, 121, 146, 158, 189, 205
Stanhouse, Don	1978-79, 1982	RHP	63, 145, 149, 189, 205
Stanicek, Pete	1987-88	IF/OF	28, 101, 127, 205
Starrette, Herm	1963-65	RHP	32, 192, 205
Stefero, John	1983, 1986	C	22, 117, 129, 205
Stephens, Gene	1960-61	OF	163, 174, 205
Stephens, Vern	1954-55	3B	47, 123, 176, 189, 205
Stephenson, Earl	1977-78	LHP	34, 205
Stephenson, Garrett	1996	RHP	34, 117, 205
Stewart, Sammy	1978-85	RHP	9, 134, 205
Stillman, Royle	1975-76	1B/DH	12, 205
Stock, Wes	1959-64	RHP	36, 52, 54, 205
Stoddard, Tim	1978-83	RHP	13, 120, 129-130, 173, 205
Stone, Dean	1963	LHP	18, 33, 169, 205
Stone, Jeff	1988	OF	18, 174, 205
Stone, Steve	1979-81	RHP	18, 50-52, 55, 57, 61, 69, 72, 76, 173, 205
Stuart, Marlin	1954	RHP	7, 9, 12, 122, 205
Sundin, Gordie	1956	RHP	32, 36, 89-90, 132, 205
Surhoff, B.J.	1996-	3B/OF	12, 28, 91, 127, 150, 188, 205
Sutcliffe, Rick	1992-93	RHP	13, 52, 66, 73, 129, 149, 182, 189, 205
Swaggerty, Bill	1983-86	RHP	116, 205
Tackett, Jeff	1991-94	C	7, 55, 67, 100, 190, 205
Tarasco, Tony	1996-97	OF	5, 189, 205
Tasby, Willie	1958-60	OF	39, 119, 169, 189, 205
Tavarez, Jesus	1998	OF	37, 205
Taylor, Dorn	1990	RHP	19, 24, 133, 205
Taylor, Joe	1958-59	OF	24, 36, 205
Telford, Anthony	1990-93	RHP	37, 189, 205
Temple, Johnny	1962	2B	19, 65, 122, 163, 167, 189, 205
Tettleton, Mickey	1988-90	C	41, 62, 89, 135, 163, 189, 205
Thomas, Valmy	1960	C	7, 180, 205
Thomson, Bobby	1960	OF	109, 118, 180, 205
Throneberry, Marv	1961-62	1B	22, 127, 172-173, 189, 205
Thurmond, Mark	1988-89	LHP	205
Tibbs, Jay	1988-90	RHP	52, 205
Torrez, Mike	1975	RHP	51, 55, 59, 189, 205
Traber, Jim	1984, 1986, 1988-89	1B	25, 101, 103, 112, 117-118, 120, 134, 189, 205
Triandos, Gus	1955-62	C	34, 37, 40, 61, 63, 74-75, 78, 92, 107, 146, 172, 178, 189, 205
Trout, Dizzy	1957	RHP	9, 127, 130, 133, 166, 176, 205
Turley, Bob	1954	RHP	12, 56, 63, 88, 146, 168, 176, 182, 205
Turner, Shane	1991	IF	19, 174, 205
Underwood, Tom	1984	LHP	127, 205
Valentine, Fred	1959, 1963, 1968	OF	21, 36, 145, 157, 169, 205
Valenzuela, Fernando	1993	LHP	16, 66, 165, 182, 205

NAME	YEARS	POS	PAGE
Van Gorder, Dave	1987	C	*167, 206*
Van Slyke, Andy	1995	OF	*15, 112, 149-150, 171, 206*
Vineyard, Dave	1964	RHP	*11, 21, 33, 206*
Virgil, Ozzie	1962	3B	*27, 79, 90, 108, 127, 180, 206*
Voigt, Jack	1992-95	OF	*206*
Waitkus, Eddie	1954-55	1B	*123, 189, 206*
Walker, Greg	1990	1B	*177, 206*
Walker, Jerry	1957-60	RHP	*48, 59, 61, 131-132, 158, 206*
Walton, Jerome	1997	OF	*182, 206*
Ward, Pete	1962	OF	*189, 206*
Warwick, Carl	1965	OF	*206*
Washington, Ron	1987	IF	*24, 189, 206*
Watt, Eddie	1966-73	RHP	*47, 112, 158, 166, 189, 206*
Webster, Lenny	1997-	C	*7, 84, 206*
Welchel, Don	1982-83	RHP	*206*
Wells, David	1996	LHP	*42, 175-176, 206*
Werley, George	1956	RHP	*89-90, 131-132, 206*
Wertz, Vic	1954	1B/OF	*107, 121, 166, 175, 189, 206*
Westlake, Wally	1955	OF	*19, 21, 36, 127, 206*
Weston, Mickey	1989-90	RHP	*206*
Whitt, Ernie	1991	C	*175, 206*
Wiggins, Alan	1985-87	2B	*20, 112, 122-123, 189, 206*
Wight, Bill	1955-57	LHP	*11, 28, 189, 206*
Wilhelm, Hoyt	1958-62	RHP	*6, 15, 41, 50, 57, 63-64, 122, 173, 180, 206*
Williams, Brian	1997	RHP	*206*
Williams, Dallas	1981	OF	*148, 206*
Williams, Dick	1956-57, 1958, 1961-62	OF/IF	*36, 136, 138-139, 142, 179, 189, 206*
Williams, Earl	1973-74	C/1B	*182, 189, 206*
Williamson, Mark	1987-93	RHP	*50, 106, 206*
Wilson, Jim	1955-56	RHP	*24, 50, 63-64, 122, 173, 176, 206*
Woodling, Gene	1955, 1958-60	OF	*36, 62, 74, 78, 107, 139, 145-146, 151, 173, 178, 189, 192, 206*
Worthington, Craig	1988-91	3B	*22, 69, 71, 155, 189, 206*
Yan, Esteban	1996-97	RHP	*22, 130, 151, 206*
Young, Bobby	1954-55	2B	*23, 36, 117, 123, 206*
Young, Mike	1982-87	OF	*41, 71, 89, 95, 102, 135, 206*
Zaun, Gregg	1995-96	C	*18, 125, 206*
Ziele, Todd	1996	3B	*206*
Zupo, Frank "Noodles"	1957-58, 1961	C	*16, 101, 112, 121, 131-132, 206*
Zuverink, George	1955-59	RHP	*56, 164, 206*